Major Conservation Issues of the 1990s

Results of the World Conservation Congress Workshops

Edited by

Jeffrey A. McNeely, Chief Scientist

Montreal, Canada
13–23 October 1996

IUCN – The World Conservation Union
1998

Published by: IUCN, Gland, Switzerland and Cambridge, UK

Copyright: © 1998, International Union for Conservation of Nature and Natural Resources

Reproduction of this publication for educational or other non-commercial purposes is authorized without prior written permission from the copyright holder provided the source is fully acknowledged.

Reproduction of this publication for resale or other commercial purposes is prohibited without prior written permission of the copyright holder.

Citation: McNeely, J.A. (Ed.) (1998). *Major Conservation Issues of the 1990s: Results of the World Conservation Congress Workshops*. IUCN, Gland, Switzerland and Cambridge, UK. vii + 203 pp.

ISBN: 2-8317-0433-2

Cover design by: Reflet Artwork for Business

Printed by: Page Brothers (Norwich) Ltd, U.K.

Available from: IUCN Publications Services Unit
                 219c Huntingdon Road, Cambridge CB3 0DL, United Kingdom
                 Tel: +44 1223 277894, Fax: +44 1223 277175
                 E-mail: iucn-psu@wcmc.org.uk
                 http://www.iucn.org
                 A catalogue of IUCN publications is also available

The text of this book is printed on Fineblade Cartridge 90 gsm paper made from low-chlorine pulp.

Foreword

This is a summary record of the proceedings of the fifty-two technical workshops and the four so-called "special events" on generic issues conducted during the first World Conservation Congress in Montreal, Canada, in October 1996.

While each workshop was organized by specific IUCN Members, Secretariat Units or partners, the overall coordination of the workshops was in the capable hands of IUCN's Chief Scientist Jeffrey A. McNeely, and he has pulled together the thematic threads – both on the spot, at the conclusion of the Montreal discussions, and in the introduction to the Proceedings below.

We are indebted to the former President of the Union, Sir Shridath Ramphal, who chaired and led with his customary flair and eloquence, the final open panel discussion of the results of the workshops. We thank also for their stimulating contributions to this wind-up debate Sir Shridath Ramphal, Marie-Angélique Savané, Julia Carabias, Keith Bezanson, Ashok Khosla and Anders Wijkman.

The workshops, all well attended and some so crowded that there was standing room only, illustrated yet again two strengths of the Union: its convening power; and the capacity of its Members and Partners to grapple with the emerging and cutting-edge aspects of the great conservation and sustainable development debates of the day.

The workshops were for the first time open to the general public. The level of participation varied but there were some very well informed and pertinent interventions from the several hundred (largely Canadian) members of the public who took part. This was an experiment which paid off.

The special events represented in essence an endeavour to widen the scope of the Union's debate about the future, to set it in some very practical contexts and to bring to the table some highly important global actors. The Union first brought governments and non-government organizations to work together – that was arguably the greatest genius shown by the founders who set up the Union almost fifty years ago. Now there is progress in bringing to the negotiating table other parties who have a major role in natural resource management and use around the world – the private sector and the financiers. Again, we are immensely grateful to the luminaries, ranging from Stephan Schmidheiny to Maurice Strong, William Ruckelshaus to Enrique Garcia and Tessa Tennant, who illustrated by their presence and views that there are several routes to sustainability and much goodwill in searching jointly for this common good.

The workshops and special events were not conducted in a vacuum. With a well organized press centre, the media at virtually all sessions and most of the programme on the Internet each day, the Congress proved to be what it was designed to be – more of a vehicle for getting out the Union's conservation messages than the old General Assemblies ever were. But the professional communicators like David Bellamy who brought their expertise and know-how to the Congress also brought home to participants how far the Union has to go in honing the communication skills which will lift its game in advocacy and wielding influence. Planning for big advances on this vital front are well underway as a result of the Montreal discussions.

It should finally be made clear that this is very much a summary only of the workshop proceedings. The many useful papers presented are not adequately reflected here, nor is the depth of discussion on each theme. This publication is designed to whet readers' appetite to delve further into the subjects covered. It should also be made clear that the conclusions reached do not always represent a Union-wide consensus on the subjects discussed. That said, I trust you will find this material stimulating and thought-provoking.

David McDowell
Director General
IUCN – The World Conservation Union

Contents

Reports from the Workshops

Stream 1: Enhancing Sustainability: Resources for the Future

Stream 2: Conserving Vitality and Diversity

Stream 3: Adapting Protected Areas Management to New Challenges

Stream 4: Sharing Nature's Bounty

Stream 10: Engaging Members and Partners

Reports from the Cross-Cutting Themes

Reports from the Special Events

Conservation towards the 21st Century
Messages from IUCN's World Conservation Congress

Jeffrey A. McNeely, Chief Scientist, IUCN – The World Conservation Union

Introduction

Conservationists are seriously concerned about economic and environmental trends around the world. Supported by the current tax and trade policies, people are consuming our planet's resources at an accelerating pace. Governments everywhere are seeking to increase labour productivity, which inevitably means more intensive use of capital, materials, and energy. Increasing resource productivity – which makes more sense from a conservation perspective – would mean reversing this trend, requiring revolutionary changes in policies on trade, technology, industry, labour, and finance. Progress toward sustainable development requires an appropriate balance between the two forms of productivity, closely linking success in conservation to the major development interests of modern society. That's why those of us who are naturalists have climbed down from our mountains, hiked out of our forests and savannas, and swam out of our coral reefs to come to IUCN's World Conservation Congress and meet with bankers, industrialists, economists, journalists, civil servants, developers, and many other interests – to seek ways of working together to influence the major global trends that are threatening the resources we are trying to maintain for future generations.

IUCN's first World Conservation Congress, held in Montreal, Canada, in October 1996, included fifty-two workshops covering a wide range of topics and drawing on a tremendous diversity of input from the 3,000 participants in the event. With hundreds of individual presentations and interventions, this wealth of input – organized largely by IUCN Members – provided a reality check for all of us, enabling us to learn what is happening in the rest of the world, and whether our activities make sense in the context of what is taking place elsewhere. The workshops gave us a chance to share our insights, information and perspectives with our colleagues from all around the world. From this great wealth of intellectual stimulation, I was asked to synthesize the major messages and new areas deserving greater attention by IUCN – its Members, Commissions, and Secretariat.

Many of us will agree that the world we want is very different from the one we are creating, and if we don't change our direction we will end up where we are heading. We need to break the "conspiracy of success" that prevents an honest assessment of experience and inhibits learning from our mistakes. Because, as one workshop pointed out, failure is the best learning experience we have, we need to risk failing, be bold in seeking solutions, learn from our failures, and build on our successes.

We heard from another workshop that a trillion dollars has been spent in official development assistance since the Second World War. That sounds like a lot of money, but in fact this is about the same amount that is being spent *every year* for inappropriate incentives. According to one United Nations estimate, governments are spending a trillion dollars a year – 50 years worth of ODA – in ways that subsidize over-exploitation of natural resources. This puts into perspective the scale of problems that we need to address, and the international financial resources that are available to address them.

A unifying theme

Many workshops suggested a unifying theme: biological diversity, or biodiversity for short. The Convention on Biological Diversity, now ratified by over 170 countries, has three objectives that are remarkably convergent with the IUCN mission statement we adopted in Buenos Aires in 1993, and which was reconfirmed here in Montreal. Our mission is: "To influence, encourage and assist societies throughout the world to conserve the integrity and diversity of nature and to ensure that any use of natural resources is equitable and ecologically sustainable". Echoing our mission, the Biodiversity Convention's objectives are "the conservation of biological diversity, the sustainable use of its components and the fair and equitable sharing of benefits arising out of the utilization of genetic resources". In giving us a framework for our programme, biodiversity brings together many different aspects of our business to form a much more comprehensive approach to conservation. It establishes a positive linkage between conservation and development that eluded us when our phrase was conservation *for* development. This linkage has enabled us to gain the attention of a far larger constituency among governments, international agencies, non-governmental organizations, and the private sector. But we still need to give much more attention to feeding the complexity of the biodiversity concept in easily-digested morsels to decision-makers and the general public who are hungry for solutions to the problems of modern society.

Levels for action

Biodiversity also implies several different levels of action, and the workshops can be conveniently regarded from these different levels. The most basic is the local level – the farm, the village, the forest, and the individual protected area. Other levels include the bioregional, the national, and the global. While action is required at all of these levels, several workshops gave particular attention to the first level, calling for local empowerment, benefits, and responsibilities. Perhaps the best attended of the workshops and in many ways the one that seemed to strike the most responsive chord among the most people, was in the form of a drama called "Guardians of Eden". The message that came out of that play seemed to boil down to four points:

❑ First, communities should be empowered to find their own solutions, requiring government policies to enable such empowerment.

❑ Second, we need to understand the past and present in order to prepare for the future.

❑ Third, seemingly-unsophisticated communities can and do make profound decisions about long-term sustainability effects on grounds that are not obviously rational in scientific terms.

❑ And fourth, and something that we must take to heart, local people are angry that those who are living far away are making decisions for them or that affect them.

Several of the workshops concluded that we must create, nurture and enable responsibility in landowners and resource users to manage and protect land and natural resources. We heard, for example, that in South Africa about 7% of the land is now in private protected areas. That is a development which needs our attention, for it is both an opportunity and a potential problem. One of the major challenges is how to build national policy support and a framework for such local initiatives and put them on a sound legal footing. You may remember part of the Hippocratic oath for physicians: first, do no harm. We have to ensure that governments do not advocate policy measures that discourage local initiatives such as these. The principle of local responsibility for local resources came up repeatedly in many of the workshops. This makes sense because feedback works especially well at the local level. When a local-level resource manager makes a mistake, he or she pays for that mistake in declining productivity of the system. When a local resource manager makes a good decision, then more benefits flow and sustainability of resource uses is more likely. Community-based management is a form of on-going natural selection, a sort of adaptive management based on real-life experience and locally-available resources.

Yet local communities are not the only bodies in society interested in managing natural resources and capable of doing so. In real-life situations it soon becomes apparent that a variety of actors – institutions, authorities, businesses, interest groups and agencies of various kinds – exist within and outside local communities. These actors have different concerns and capacities to bring forward, which should not be "lumped" together, not even into an (improbable) "community position". As discussed in the workshop on collaborative management, various actors can assume different responsibilities and receive different benefits for the ultimate advantage of both conservation and society. Such partnerships require much time and resources to develop and are dependent on genuine professional commitment, but they assure the best chances for the sustainability of conservation and effective resource management.

Many of the workshops also stressed the importance of indigenous knowledge. The democratic trends that we see in many parts of the world have reinforced the legitimacy of tribal and communal responsibility over many areas. Native title in one form or another has been recognized or reinstated at least partially in Brazil, Colombia, Australia, New Zealand, Canada, and many other countries. But at the same time, we also heard that traditional knowledge should be on the list of endangered species. Of the world's 6,000 languages at least half are no longer being taught to young people, so we are losing cultural diversity even more quickly than we are losing biological diversity. This means that we are losing a significant part of the knowledge that people have learned over many generations for adapting to their local ecosystems.

One of the problems has been that the local knowledge has been freely used by anybody who can get ahold of it. A study that was quoted from UNDP suggested that the developing world would gain around US$5.4 billion per year if multinational food, seed and pharmaceutical firms paid royalties for local knowledge and plant varieties. While such calculations are highly speculative, that amount of money could make a real difference to local communities, if spent appropriately.

We also need to address conservation at the bioregional scale. By my count, at least eight workshops converged on this level. Protected areas must not be islands surrounded by hostile land uses, because they are never large enough to protect all the natural processes, such as evolution or predator-prey relations, that they are designed to conserve. They need to be managed as part of a larger regional landscape – what is called in many parts of the world a biosphere reserve, or in the UK a national park. A broader bioregion that is managed for purposes compatible with the Convention on Biological Diversity can be relevant to mountain systems, marine systems, wetland systems, arid lands, and any other biome. We need to find a scale large enough to deal with the complexity of the systems involved, but small enough to enable the people involved to come together to negotiate solutions to the critical conflicts that must be resolved.

The national level we all know very well as where sovereignty is lodged, where binding decisions are made in the interest of all a nation's citizens. But national governments everywhere are under pressure today and most of their budgets are declining in real terms. Less money is available from central governments to support the kinds of activities we all care about, so we need to focus more on the highest priorities: what really needs to happen first at the national government level to enable real progress to follow at all the other levels? We need to stimulate more appropriate action at the national level, especially where IUCN members in each country can come together to put pressure on the political system toward agreed conservation objectives. One place to start may be to redirect that trillion dollars per year of perverse incentives toward more positive ends, thereby both saving money and conserving biodiversity.

And finally, we need to work, as we are doing at this Congress, at the international or the global level. One of the recurring themes throughout the workshops was a focus on international programmes and conventions. If we examine the list of international conventions that are relevant to our business, the Convention on Biological Diversity is at the top of the list. Recall that we originated this Convention back at the Third World Congress on National Parks in Bali in 1982, and developed it further through the efforts of the Environmental Law Centre of IUCN and several IUCN General Assemblies before feeding it into the intergovernmental process. The Biodiversity Convention is ours. It says the kinds of things that we need governments to say, and its objectives re-state the IUCN mission. Now that governments have agreed to it, it is time to implement it on the ground, and that remains a big challenge for all of us.

The Convention on International Trade in Endangered Species has also been a very prominent concern, not only in workshops about species, but also those on trade and the environment, addressing issues such as fisheries and forests as well as more traditional wildlife. The Law of the Sea Convention has many aspects that are relevant to our activities in the coastal and marine environments. The Convention on Wetlands of International Importance is very closely linked to our work on wetlands. The World Heritage Convention, which next year will be celebrating its 25th anniversary, is designed to give special attention to areas of global importance, areas where we should all invest some of our time and effort. The Desertification Convention, which has not received nearly the attention that it should from IUCN, will be coming into force at the end of this year, and is especially relevant to Africa, where the problems of sustainable use of wildlife species, vegetation, fisheries, and water, are especially critical. As we heard from another workshop, the Climate Change Convention can support more effective management of protected areas, but it also affects issues like invasive species, coral reefs, biodiversity, and wetlands.

All of these international negotiations are central to our work. The people who are representing governments at the negotiating table, however, are seldom as well briefed as they should be about our concerns. Negotiators at the Climate Change Convention do not understand the importance of their Convention for biological diversity, protected areas, or marine conservation. They may have been briefed about trade issues for the World Trade Organization, but are they informed about the impact of trade on the environment? We need to take advantage of the opportunities these conventions provide at the global level to get better performance out of our national governments.

But at the same time, what about governments that are already over-stretched? Governments have less money available for the environment, yet we have a proliferation of international environmental conventions requiring seemingly-endless meetings. The documentation for the Convention on Biological Diversity held in Argentina the week after the WCC was over 15 centimetres thick! What government has enough resources the enable its relevant staff to even read all of that material, much less respond to it in a thoughtful way? And that's only one of the conventions. Like the ticking of a metronome, or a time bomb, meetings of Conventions, Panels, and Programmes keep coming one after another. We are in real danger of spending all of our time talking to each other, reading papers, and going to international meetings. What can we do to streamline this international programme – this international proliferation of very useful and very important legislation? One suggestion made by Maurice Strong is that we should have a World Environment Organization that would bring all of these different pieces of legislation together in a more comprehensive way and help enable governments to respond in a more productive manner. These multiple obligations are in danger of becoming a burden, and if they become a burden to governments they won't be implemented – an outcome that would represent a tragic lost opportunity.

That said, we also need to recognize that the negotiation process has been very useful for the conservation movement, bringing our concerns to the attention of governments and political leaders (with all the risks attending such exposure). For example, the policy dialogue known as the Intergovernmental Panel on Forests certainly is influencing national forest policies, so we need to influence our national delegations to those discussions and use them to further our conservation interests.

One last global point: the global economy means that we are now globally tied together in a global market. If you walk down the street in Montreal you can buy goods from just about anywhere in the world. It can be 40° below zero outside, and you can still purchase fresh tomatoes. This is wonderful. But what happens back where those tomatoes are being grown? The consumers of the traded tomatoes here in Montreal don't have any idea – there's no feedback loop between the global economy and the local production of the resources, between the way those resources are being managed on the ground and the way that we're consuming at the global level. We need to build better feedback into our system so that consumers are made aware of the environmental impacts of their consumption. We also should be aware that global economic integration increases the chances of sudden and rapid economic destabilization. If we all become highly dependent on global forces over which nobody seems to have much control, the whole system could unravel like a cheap sweater and we could face unprecedented problems whose solutions may well come from the locally-available resources and knowledge we are able to conserve.

Emerging issues

The workshops identified numerous emerging issues. One of the most interesting was the **increased emphasis given to people**. We need to consider many different social classes, groups, and both genders in the work that we are doing. Why is that? The benefits from using resources historically have been flowing to the wealthier sectors: the export producers, the commercial farmers, the investors in extractive industries. But the costs have been shouldered especially by the poor, by subsistence farmers, the informal sector workers, and women. Women throughout all societies and at all levels have often been left out of the environmental equation – their actual and potential contribution, the consequences of their behaviour, and the potential effects of environmental activities on their lives and livelihoods have been ignored. So a special effort was made during the Congress to introduce **gender perspectives** and the need for gender analysis, and a Gender Resource Team was formed to monitor the integration. This exercise showed that we still have a long way to go. Some workshops did discuss empowerment of the real resource users, both men and women, calling on conservation to include the most marginalized and to understand the differences not only between the genders but also within them. And while some workshops made a passing reference to projects involving women, serious discussions of gender issues in most was conspicuously absent. We have not yet understood that we need a fundamental re-thinking of our approach to conservation, not a simple "add on" of projects or project elements for women. We have not yet realized that ignoring the importance of gender-determined roles is detrimental to both our conservation efforts and to the men and women of the communities with which we interact.

Issues of **equity** and the **collaborative management** approaches that were discussed in many workshops provide powerful pathways towards both a more effective and efficient management of natural resources and a more just and equitable sharing of the benefits arising from this improved management. We should keep in mind, however, that the richest 350 people in the world control capital assets that are equivalent to those held by the poorest 50% of the world's population. We have a long way to go to correct the inequities that characterize today's world.

Apart from equity issues, it is evident that when people are not involved in reaching decisions, the chances of their compliance are slim. And yet powerful mechanisms are available to involve various actors in collaborative management partnerships. Collaborative management agreements can take many forms, including active consultation of stakeholders, negotiation of a specific share of rights and responsibilities, involvement in a formal management body, partial devolution of functions, and so on. Only the relevant actors can identify the approach best suited to the context at stake.

Other workshops examined **why resources are being over-consumed**. In one workshop economists told us that global resources are being consumed especially by citizens of countries that have very well defined property rights, and resources are over-produced (that is, depleted) especially by those countries with ill-defined property rights. As a result, the full costs of production are being ignored – in economic terms, these costs are "externalized". The system has no feedback, so it cannot adapt to change. If economic factors are leading to over-exploitation, then we need to correct these institutional failures through mobilizing economic tools for conserving biodiversity. For better or worse, economics is now the language of discourse of decision makers, so we must learn to use the language of economists. If we are able to quantify the economic value of water-based ecosystems, for example, and to specify the role of those systems in supporting local communities downstream, then decision makers may be able to see the wisdom of conservation upstream and enact the laws that provide an appropriate property rights regime.

We heard many good examples of things that are working, at least in some places. One of the most interesting was **restoration ecology**. "Restoration ecology" may sound as if it's rather abstract science, but the workshop that addressed the subject said: "Restoration ecology allows people an opportunity for personal self-transformation, community renewal and a way to resonate with the ancient traditions of world renewal". Thus ecologists, too, are beginning to see that conservation is a social movement, calling for profound cultural change.

Many of the workshops discussed the dynamism of systems. We heard that the protected area systems of the world are constantly changing. A report from one part of the world said that they hope "to complete the protected areas system by the year 2000". But I don't believe we should think in terms of ever completing protected area systems, because conditions are dynamic. With climate change, changing patterns of land use, and changing economic systems, protected areas too will constantly change. And we don't need to devote much time to discussing whether they should cover 10% or 12% or 15% of the landscape. What really matters is the way that we manage the entire landscape, the way that protected areas relate to the surrounding lands. If we manage our lands well, a protected area estate of 10% is ample, but if we abuse the rest of our landscape, then 15% is not nearly enough.

We heard a lot about ecosystem management, which is strongly endorsed by the CBD, but the regulatory mechanisms used in most countries are often very species-specific. CITES, endangered species laws, and many sustainable use programmes are all aimed at individual species or populations, so we need to complement the ecosystem approach with improved approaches to species conservation. And surely one of the most interesting products for the general public is the **Red List of Endangered Species**. The release of the latest edition the week before the WCC attracted tremendous attention and people started to renew their concern about what is happening to the species on the Red List. Given the communications power of such tools, it was suggested that they should be extended to ecosystems as well.

All the workshops addressed the cross-cutting issue of **communications**, either directly or indirectly. It is clear that communications are critical to building a broader constituency. We need clear communications, influential input from the stakeholders, and apparent and obvious support for the initiatives of other interests and other ways of ensuring that people understand the processes, the results and the impact of the conservation initiatives that we're trying to push.

We also heard from the people who are working on **information and electronic communication technology**, one of the most dramatic innovations of the late 20th century. Here is what they say: "Many information technologies are available and are being used by IUCN members and partners. Now is a good time to get started as the conservation community has people who can help give advice on which are best to use". Perhaps IUCN could offer a useful service by providing a framework for packaging conservation information into easily digested and applied portions. Indeed, the newly-created Biodiversity Conservation Information System, bringing together the efforts of several parts of the greater IUCN family, is an important step in this direction.

We also talked a lot about **trade and the environment**, and especially about how we can work more productively with **the private sector**. Over the past few years, official development assistance has been declining slowly, while private sector investment has been growing so quickly that it is now by far the dominant player in developing countries (though the vast majority of this investment is in about 15 rapidly-industrializing countries, while most others are largely ignored by private investors). As one indication of their economic influence, the ten largest multinational corporations now have sales that exceed the combined GNP of the 100 smallest countries. The private sector is also the primary vehicle for transmitting cultural values through advertising, cinema and popular music. These facts indicate that a constructive cross-sectoral dialogue is needed between business and conservation, based on mutual interests in the sustainability of resource use. We need to encourage industry to move beyond compliance and risk management and into building conservation principles into their corporate planning as a strategic opportunity.

But a question that will be on all of our minds is, who will be able to oblige the private sector to internalize its social and environmental costs, especially when these cross national borders?

Conclusions: What IUCN can do

So what kind of a future do we want? Here are ten suggestions on what IUCN can do, seeking to synthesize the key messages from the 52 workshops into just a few words.

❑ First, we need to build a stronger constituency through providing or publicizing the benefits of conservation to more people and interest groups. We need to develop partnerships by which the benefits and responsibilities of conservation are equitably shared in society.

❑ Second, we need to help raise conservation issues and define what should be the public priorities. This will depend on improved communications with multiple audiences on subjects that have eluded media attention, such as how biodiversity loss and ecological degradation affect and are affected by cultural loss, poverty and human disease, and the linkages between trade and the environment.

❑ Third, we need to provide a forum for discussions of issues that are not yet on the international agenda, for example the impact of decentralization on biodiversity, underlying causes of threats to biodiversity, issues of land tenure, unsustainable consumption, and even the impact of corruption on conservation.

❑ Fourth, we need to give more attention to invasive alien species and restoration ecology, the former as a major conservation challenge and the latter as a major conservation opportunity.

❑ Fifth, we need to provide positive examples of best practice, including self-reliance, gender issues, and equity. And perhaps we need also to provide bad examples or good examples of bad practice. We need to work on monitoring and evaluating successes, failures, and trends, leading us in productive new directions.

❑ Sixth, we need to greatly expand our use of legal and economic tools for conservation, including economic incentives, green taxes, charges, compensation, debt relief, environmental funds, and many others. Couching our positions in economic terms will enhance our credibility with politicians and other decision-makers.

❑ Seventh, we need to provide scientifically credible information that is readily accessible to the public and to policy makers and in a form they can use – another task for information technology and communications.

❑ Eighth, we need to promote productive new partnerships between different sectors, between governments and NGOs, between the private and public sectors, and between different scientific disciplines. We need to help promote institutional and intellectual hybrid vigour.

❑ Ninth, we need to find ways to promote a diversity of solutions to local conservation problems, support more effective national conservation policies, and use global conventions and other measures to give greater legitimacy to conservation action on the ground.

❑ And finally, we need to do what we did at the World Conservation Congress: promote and facilitate exchanges of views, and help to get people in touch with each other so that they can pursue their own diverse interests and concerns more effectively.

In short, we need action that is economically practical, ecologically sound, politically palatable, socially acceptable, and legally enforceable. That of course will require site-specific responses in each individual country, built on sound national policy and supported by vigorous international cooperation. We need to look for incremental improvements, not to expect revolutionary changes necessarily, but to continue to take significant steps along the way toward a more sustainable future. We need to combine a rigorous scientific analysis with the socio-economic and spiritual values embraced by society to shape a landscape that can adapt to the changes that the 21st century will surely bring.

Reports from the
Workshops

1.1 Enhancing Sustainability: Resources for the Future

Organizer: IUCN/SSC Sustainable Use Initiative

Chair: John Robinson, Chair SUI Advisory Group; Vice-President, Wildlife Conservation Society

Rapporteur: Peter Gillespie

Summary

*This workshop comprised five technical sessions: a) an introductory plenary where the topic of sustainable use was introduced; b) three thematic sessions highlighting sustainable use issues relevant to artisanal fisheries, community-based management of forests and management of wildlife for sustainable use; and c) a closing session during which key lessons learned from each of the sessions were discussed. The three thematic sessions were organized by Regional Sustainable Use Specialist Groups: West Africa – artisanal fisheries; Central America – community-based management of forests; and North America – management of wildlife for sustainable use. A special session, organized by the Southern African Sustainable Use Specialist Group, was a play entitled **Guardians of Eden**. A brief summary, overview and list of papers and/or presentations for each of the first five sessions of the workshop are presented below. In the interest of space, the chief conclusions of the closing session are presented in the overview of the workshop. Also, the output and follow-up for individual sessions have been consolidated in the overview of the workshop. With the exception of the presentation of **Guardians of Eden**, discussions were facilitated by the rapporteur, ensuring that all participants were given the opportunity to express their views.*

Objectives

1. To summarize regional perspectives on sustainable use of renewable natural resources.

2. To identify global principles of sustainable use.

3. To review the changing understanding of the concept of sustainable use.

4. To highlight selected global issues related to the concept of sustainable use.

5. To provide a vision for the future of the IUCN/SSC Sustainable Use Initiative.

Conclusions

The variability and multiplicity of biological, institutional and socio-economic factors, none of which in itself is a good indicator of sustainability, means that it is the interaction among the factors that matters. Given that certain relationships do permit generalizations, the Sustainable Use Initiative will present these in a policy statement and will make the application of regionally-derived analyses a priority in the forthcoming triennium. The challenge for the Sustainable Use Initiative is to ensure that the results of the analyses can influence the policy process.

Understanding the sustainable use concept

Key points regarding understanding of the concept of sustainable use:

1. Management of nature depends on the process by which we can understand the nature of nature, and the impacts of human policy decisions on that nature (the analytical element); the political process that generates policies for natural resource management (the political element); and the interactions between the two.

2. Sustainable use is not determinate – a multitude of configurations of biological, social and economic factors influence the sustainability of uses of wild renewable resources. Sustainability lies not in the factors themselves but in the manner in which these factors interact and influence each other.

3. The debate about sustainable use notwithstanding, the concept can: a) involve consumptive commercial use; b) be an alternative to protected areas; c) involve indigenous peoples and local communities; and d) give resources economic value.

4. While wildlife has value it is a public resource belonging to everyone. Therefore, uncontrolled use of wildlife is unacceptable. But use of wildlife can be controlled. Government intervention is needed to conserve wildlife for future generations, and wildlife populations can be perpetuated indefinitely while sustained use is occurring.

5. Today we recognize that there is a limit to the extent that protected areas alone can achieve in conserving nature over time. We also know that the local people, who were considered part of the problem, are now considered part of the solution in community based conservation. The long-term solution is found in partnerships between states (regulations), research institutions (scientific knowledge), and users (local knowledge, inputs to decision-making).

6. Crises resulting from over-exploitation are often the pre-condition to improving management. Progress toward more sustainable development carries two prices:

    ❏ **Economic:** Where consumptive, commercial utilization of a wild resource is central to off-setting the opportunity costs of alternate land/water uses, the resource must command a high price, but this risks over-exploitation of high value species and overspecialization in production of high-value species at the expense of natural biodiversity.

    ❏ **Over-reliance:** An over-reliance on consumptive, commercial utilization can be dangerous because: a) the use may be uncompetitive with alternate land/water uses; b) dependence on a few wild species commodities increases the risk that both values/ markets and ecosystems/ populations will change unpredictability; and c) economic specialization can lead to eco-system simplification.

7. In the long term, biodiversity conservation will require fundamental changes in the way we account for, pay for, and manage different values associated with wild renewable natural resources. Economic sanctions on countries are a blunt instrument with unintended side effects (e.g., sanctions against Canadian fur trade).

8. Governments should devolve at least some responsibility for resource management to communities, who will then "own" and protect their resources. Sustainable use practices should:

    ❏ use a biological knowledge base and adaptive management;

    ❏ recognize the right of rural communities and local people to access natural resources;

    ❏ involve communities and the local people in the design, implementation and monitoring of resource management plans;

    ❏ be encouraged by ensuring economic benefits to rural people and local communities; and

    ❏ stress the importance of adaptive management, recognizing that in most wild resource management systems there is incomplete *a priori* knowledge (about the resource, and social and economic factors that will influence its sustainability).

    Therefore, institutionalized mechanisms are needed in the management system that facilitate adaptation to changes as experience unfolds and new information becomes available.

9. Sustainable development and human development need to be better integrated by strengthening institutions at both national and local levels. In concrete terms, environmental conservation needs to be balanced by the need to enhance living conditions of people – or suffer from social inequality, political instability, poverty, and inability to advance sustainable development. Rural communities which are empowered to manage their own affairs can lead to other community initiatives, including conservation of biodiversity at the local level. In general, it is important that land reform be negotiated with rural communities. However, at the national level, moves to decentralize land-use decisions pose challenges in balancing local focus on short-term benefits with the presumed interests of future generations. It is important to find ways to adjust different land tenure schemes to the different circumstances at the local level.

SUI agenda for the future

The approach of the Sustainable Use Initiative to enhance understanding of the concept of "sustainable use" has five strategic roots:

1. a **systematic approach** to correct the fragmented, bio-centric and often species-specific foci;

2. an **experimental methodological approach** to enhancing understanding, with its emphasis on testable hypotheses, grounded data, dialectic between management experience and policy, and continuous adaptation;

3. the importance of effective and efficient **regulatory mechanisms** to control use, balancing incentives and disincentives;

4. **decentralized structures** for implementing SUI;

5. **devolution of authority** to reflect the spectrum of the Union's membership: i) correcting the imbalance now favouring the economically highly-developed countries; and ii) addressing the dissonance between international initiatives with low accountability, where those making recommendations are not accountable for their implementation contexts.

These strategic roots will continue to guide the future development of the SUI. The SUI will decentralize further by forming new regional specialist groups. The Initiative will continue the devolution process by providing a global secretariat to support the process, maintaining a close-knit executive unit, electing the Chair of the Sustainable Use Specialist Group Steering Committee by the Steering Committee members, and examining further the executive direction of SUI.

SUI will continue to focus on analysis of those factors which enhance or detract from the sustainability of resource use. In this context the SUI will tailor the scope of its agenda within IUCN to systemic demand rather than topical boundaries which lead to competitive agendas, waste of resources and dissonance between need and demand. The SUI will strive for greater cohesion with other programmes and initiatives at the international level on matters of global significance.

There was an appeal to IUCN to more forcefully demonstrate how sustainable use tools can be applied to real-life situations. If the Union takes this step, political support will follow. The SUI is developing the scientific and technological expertise thorough its global network to provide a service to advise on practical sustainable-use issues. Furthermore, IUCN can influence issues at the global level and in individual countries if it accepts this challenge.

Cross-cutting issues

In addition to the stated objectives of each workshop session, participants were invited to comment specifically on the "role of women" in relation to sustainable use of renewable natural resources. There was consensus that women were crucial in enhancing the sustainability of uses of wild resources at the community level; that their participation in resource management/conservation activities and in the decision-making bodies overseeing the management was essential. There was also recognition of the role women play in educating and training children in rural communities. While women are not always observed as being an integral part of community-based wildlife management programmes they probably are having considerable influence. Therefore, it was agreed that the percent of women observed participating in a management programme is not necessarily a reliable indicator of the role women are in fact performing.

Outputs and Follow-up

❏ The IUCN/SSC Sustainable Use Initiative will develop a sustainable use policy statement for submission to IUCN Council and circulation to members.

❏ The IUCN/SSC Sustainable Use Initiative will develop more effective means to contribute to policy issues related to sustainable use.

❏ Effort will be given to enhancing and mobilizing the capacities of the existing regional Sustainable Use Specialist Groups to contribute to advise and assist national, regional and global institutions concerned with the sustainability of uses of wild renewable resources.

❏ Greater effort will be given to collaboration with other IUCN programmes and interested partners to enhance understanding of the concept of sustainable use.

❏ *A Sustainable Use Technical Series* will be launched by the IUCN/SSC Sustainable Use Initiative to promote more effective communications. The first volume will include most of the papers presented in the workshop sessions.

❏ *Sustainable Use Policy Briefs* will be prepared summarizing selected factors which influence national, regional and global policies pertaining to sustainable use. (e.g., tenure, common property, rural incentive systems).

Papers and Presentations

1. Evolving Understanding of Sustainable Use (John Robinson, Chair SUI Advisory Group; Vice President, Wildlife Conservation Society, USA)

2. Strategic Roots and Implementational Evolution: Considerations for the Future in the Sustainable Use Initiative (Marshall Murphree, SUI Advisory Group, Chair IUCN/SSC Sustainable Use Specialist Group. Director, Centre for Applied Social Sciences, University of Zimbabwe, Zimbabwe)

3. What Price for Sustainability? (Curt Freese, WWF-International, USA)

4. Investment in People - A Key to Enhance Sustainability: Lessons from Northern Pakistan (Javed Ahmed, Head of Natural Resources Group, IUCN Pakistan and Shoab Sultan, Senior Advisor of Rural Development, UNDP, Pakistan)

5. Tenure Issues Related to Sustainability (Shem Migot-Adhola, The World Bank, USA)

6. Sustainable Use and Global Issues (Leif Christoffersen, Consultant, USA).

1.2 Sustainability in Artisanal Fisheries

Organizer: Thomas Price, IUCN Niger

Co-Chairs: Ambouta Karimou, Interim Chair, West Africa Sustainable Use Specialist Group; Thayer Scudder, Professor of Anthropology, California Institute of Technology.

Rapporteur: Peter Gillespie

Summary

Case studies were used to identify and examine various factors that are influencing the sustainability of artisanal fisheries in West Africa. The principal conclusions reached include: a) artisanal fishermen are key actors in the management of coastal zones; b) artisanal fisheries are traditionally managed through a system of lineage-based rights of individuals to fish and to control fishing; and c) artisanal fisheries should be considered in integrated coastal zone planning along with commercial fishing, tourism, agriculture, transport, urbanization, and conservation. Ways need to be found for IUCN, for example through the Sustainable Use Initiative, to collaborate with governments and institutions to enlighten them on decision-making choices regarding artisanal fisheries and their consequences of those different choices.

Objectives

1. To highlight sustainable use issues in relation to artisanal fisheries in West Africa.
2. To compare the West African experience of artisanal fisheries with other regions of the world.

Conclusions

The entire region of West Africa is facing reductions of fish stocks, degradation of the environment and human population growth pressures that are having negative impacts on the rural economies and the life styles of rural people. Sustainable use is seen as a solution involving partnerships between states (regulators), research institutions (scientific and technical knowledge) and users (local knowledge, inputs to decision-making). Involvement of all key stakeholders (including fishermen, local authorities, etc.) in understanding the factors and fish management choices has led to the development of draft legislation that is strongly supported by some governments in West Africa.

Artisanal fishermen are key actors in the management of coastal zones. As such they should be recognized as knowledgeable managers of the coastal resources. Their concerns should be respected. Special rights should be provided to resident fishermen to fish. In this regard, it is important to make available to foreign interests areas not assigned to local fishermen. Residents will then defend "their" resource and "their" environment.

Artisanal fisheries are traditionally managed through a system of lineage-based rights of individuals to fish and to control fishing. With the arrival of new technologies, fish species are being depleted. There have been various attempts in West Africa to promote modern fishing policies concurrently with traditional systems of fisheries management under a decentralized arrangement. Such systems have often been managed by individuals who lacked technical backgrounds in fisheries, leading to unsatisfactory results. Today, there is a trend in the region to empower local people to manage and use fisheries resources.

It is important that artisanal fisheries be considered in integrated coastal zone planning along with commercial fishing, tourism, agriculture, transport, urbanization, and conservation.

Ways need to be found for IUCN, for example through the SUI, to collaborate with governments and institutions to enlighten them on decision-making choices regarding artisanal fisheries and their consequences of those different choices. The identification of mitigating measures in terms of the impact of dams on biodiversity conservation and their costs and consequences is of particular importance to the maintenance of traditional artisanal fisheries and the sustainability of such fisheries.

Papers and Presentations

1. Introduction/Opening Comments. (Ambouta Karimou, Interim Chair, SUI West Africa SUSG, and Dean, Faculty of Agriculture, Abdou Moumouni University, Niger; and Thayer Scudder, USA).

2. Le rôle du savoir traditionnel dans la gestion des pêcheries du delta intérieur du Niger au Mali. (Kassibo Bréhima, Anthropoligue, Institut d'Economie Rurale, Mali).

3. Les organisations professionelles et la pêche durable en Afrique de l'Ouest. (Kobla Amegavie, Initiatives Développement Pêche, Togo).

4. Pêche artisanale et conservation du littoral en Afrique de l'Ouest. (Pierre Campredon, Secrétaire exécutif, Foundation Internationale du Banc d'Arguin, France).

5. La gestion durable des pêcheries dans l'Archipel des Bijagos et dans le Rio Grande de Buba. (Domingos de Barros, Directeur Général de la Pêche Artisanale, Guinea- Bissau).

1.3 Community-based Management of Forests

Organizer: Nestor Windevoxhel, IUCN Regional Office for Meso-America, Costa Rica

Chair: Juan Carlos Godoy, Interim Chair, Central America Sustainable Use Specialist Group

Rapporteur: Peter Gillespie

Summary

Key lessons from the workshop session are: community participation in the benefits of resource use and in the policy-making processes enhance sustainability; economic considerations, particularly constraints to accessing markets, can have a negative influence on the sustainability of a use; community access to resource rights is a critical factor; and communities must assume long-term responsibility for managing their resources.

Objectives

1. To compile, analyze, and disseminate information on sustainable use of forest resources.

2. To improve the knowledge of IUCN constituents and the general public on sustainable use of forest resources.

3. To communicate the necessary knowledge to build the capacity of IUCN members and the general public on these issues.

Conclusions

The case studies that were presented highlighted several key points that have broader relevance:

1. The Central American Council for Development and the Environment has requested information and technical input about sustainable use, demonstrating the importance of having an institutional capacity in IUCN to promote greater understanding of sustainable use. There was agreement on the value of supporting specific projects involving sustainable use that can serve as demonstrations at regional level. It is crucial that such projects be field-oriented and implemented with local participation. In such projects it is also important that rural peoples and/or communities participate in the decision-making processes from the onset of project design as well as in the implementation of the project. Women need to be involved in the decision-making processes.

2. In Brazil, the government has not yet committed itself to community participation in the management of forests. Officials tend to neglect biodiversity conservation while focusing on

products derived from uses of wild renewable natural resources.

3. Community-based management of mangroves in Matang, Malaysia and the Sundarbans of India/Pakistan demonstrate that sustainable use works over very long periods. Mangrove logging has been used to demonstrate the value of using traditional knowledge in establishing management practices. Nevertheless, inadequate community participation still prevails in the region. Sustainable use practices by rural communities need to be encouraged by ensuring that economic benefits from managed uses of renewable natural resources go to local communities.

4. A community-based management programme for Roneraies Palm (*Borassus aethiopium*) in Niger demonstrated how active village involvement in managing their resources has resulted in their commitment to conserve other species and to invest in the regeneration of the natural habitat. The project also demonstrates the importance of balancing the role of the state with participation of rural people.

5. In Belize plans for forest harvests need to be based on a legal framework that protects both the resource itself and biodiversity. Further, natural forest management should be based on an improved understanding of the ecological processes of the forest. It is essential that such planning identify and protect all species in the ecosystem that need protection, not just those that are being harvested. The challenge in forest management is to balance four interacting elements of sustainable use: ecological, economic, social/cultural, and institutional/political.

Based on the case studies, participants agreed on the need for governments to devolve responsibility for resource management to communities, who will then "own" and protect the resources. Also, rural communities should be more involved in the practical aspects of management of renewable natural resources. Commercial activities such as logging and tourism can be used to demonstrate the economic benefits that can be derived from uses of wild renewable natural resources to local communities.

The workshop agreed that sustainable use practices should promote:

❑ mechanisms for both local and private sector access to resources;

❑ more efficient access to markets;

❑ active promotion in rural communities, including means to use the knowledge and practices of local communities; and

❑ concrete examples of successful sustainable use activities that are authoritatively documented.

Papers and Presentations

1. Introduction/Opening Comments (Juan Carlos Godoy, Interim Chair, Central America Sustainable Use Specialist Group, Guatemala)

2. Gestión Comunitaria y Sostenible de los Bosques en América Central (Alberto Salas, IUCN Regional Office for Meso-America, Costa Rica)

3. Sustainable Management of Mangrove Forests in Asia (Zakir Hussain, Head, IUCN Thailand)

4. Sustainable Use of Mangroves in Central America (Alejandro Imbach, IUCN Regional Office for Meso-America, Costa Rica and Nestor Windevoxhel, IUCN Regional Office for Meso-America, Costa Rica)

5. Rôles et place des communautés villageoises dans la conservation et l'utilisation durable des resources forestières. (Salay Gambo, Coordinateur du programme, Niger)

6. La Experiencia del Plan Piloto Forestal de Quintana Roo, México, en Relación al Uso Sostenible de Recursos (Alberto Vargas, University of Wisconsin, USA)

7. Sustainable Timber Harvesting in Belize: The Columbia Controlled Felling Programme (Virginia Vasquez, Belize)

8. Community Forestry in South America (Eduardo Mansur, IUCN Regional Office for South America, Ecuador).

1.4 Guardians of Eden

Coordinator: Michael Murphree, Southern Africa Sustainable Use Specialist Group, Zimbabwe

Chair: Rowan Martin, Chair, Southern Africa Sustainable Use Specialist Group

Summary

*The play, **Guardians of Eden**, underscored three key lessons: Communities can and should be empowered to find their own solutions; it is important to understand the past and present in order to prepare for the future; and seemingly unsophisticated communities make profound decisions in relation to long-term sustainability of wild natural resource management on grounds that are not obviously economic, nor necessarily rational to someone outside of their culture. The play showed African attitudes and perspectives to natural resources and their management, and the historical process of man/natural resources interactions in Africa.*

Objectives

1. To introduce theatre as a new tool in IUCN circles for communicating African perspectives on sustainable use issues.

2. To dramatize issues of sustainable use of wildlife in Africa.

Conclusions

Guardians of Eden is a play about African villagers and resource management. Summoned by a great spirit medium, representatives from rural villages in several African countries come together to discuss their survival. Their world is changing, they are gravely concerned about the degradation of their land and they seek a direction for development in the future. They decide first to review the history of their land and natural resources before they are ready to deal with the issues facing them – in the manner of a very artistic scenario of evolution in Africa from the age of the dinosaurs up to the time of modern wildlife and humans. Having set the stage, the main theme of the play is told in traditional style through a parable. The parable centres around an older chief who gathers his three sons around him and tells them they must challenge each other for leadership of the village. But before they are ready to do this, they must go out into the wide world which lies beyond their village and return in three months with ideas which will give the village a sound basis for development and enhance their future prosperity.

The days of the old chief are numbered. He will not be present to see the outcome of the progress of his sons in a confusing world of politicians, bureaucrats, international donors, NGOs and sharp businessmen. But he has left instructions on how the village affairs are to be conducted when his sons return and, through the influence of the spirit medium and the women of the village, the parable has an exciting climax.

The play provided several lessons about the use of the medium as a communications tool:

1. Theatre provides a way to bridge the communications gap between people from different parts of the world with diverse points of view.

2. Communications benefits can be extended and deepened by:

   ❑ Providing feedback to the countries and peoples that contributed to the play's development on comparable experiences and lessons learned in other parts of the world;

   ❑ The actors in the play will bring back new skills to contribute to the growth of theatre in their own communities; and

   ❑ The use of this medium can be used to promote the "sustainable use" and "conservation" messages promoted in other countries.

3. Theatre can be very effective in "loosening up people's thinking" in relation to their own behaviours and choices in relation to sensitive topics such as sustainable use.

4. IUCN should make more use of theatre to reach more audiences, and to deepen its impact on those it now reaches through conventional means.

Papers and Presentations

1. Introduction (Rowan Martin, Chair Southern Africa Sustainable Use Specialist Group, Zimbabwe).

2. Guardians of Eden (Theatre for Africa Group, South Africa Cast of Players: Actress/Presenter Liz Ellenbogen, Actor/Presenter Ndlandla Mavundla, Actor/Presenter Raymond Kasawaya, Actor/Presenter Mandla Moyo, Actor/Presenter Jonathan Muthubi, Actor/Presenter Samson Felo, Actor/Presenter Msatero Tembo, Technical Support: Renier Keyser, Rowan Martin, Yvonne Dadla, Mike Murphree).

3. Presentation by the producer Nicholas Ellenbogen, Theatre for Africa, South Africa.

1.5 Managing Wildlife for Sustainable Use

Organizer: Rick Parsons, Safari Club International, USA; Donald MacLauchlan, International Association of Fish and Wildlife Agencies, USA

Chair: James Teer, Interim Chair, North America Sustainable Use Specialist Group

Rapporteur: Peter Gillespie

Summary

Observations from case studies:

1. *Each wildlife management situation has unique variables that influence the sustainability of the management regime.*

2. *Conservation of biodiversity is achieved primarily through landowner incentives.*

3. *A key to the recovery of depleted wildlife populations is cooperation between governments and users.*

4. *Compatibility of national and international policies concerning management and sustainable use of wildlife is important.*

5. *Incentives to manage wildlife and motivations influencing government expenditures for wildlife management vary according to the target species. Factors that seem to be important are: whether the wildlife resource is of recreational importance; whether the species has gained public support for its conservation; whether the species is important to rural communities for subsistence; and the prospect for mangers and/or landowner and the government can realize revenue from the use.*

6. *Individual ownership and/or rights of access to wildlife species have significant impact on the conservation of the species.*

7. *Involvement of local people varied between the management regimes showcased and, therefore, may or may not have an impact on conservation; and*

8. *Many uses of wildlife are sustainable.*

Objectives

1. To demonstrate different contexts in which natural resources are managed and used in different regions of the world.

2. To describe the commonalities of sustainable use of wildlife in different regions of the world.

3. To present the case for managing wildlife and associated natural resources where indigenous peoples depend on wildlife resources for their sustenance and even survival.

4. To demonstrate the concept of sustainable use as a strategy for long-term conservation.

Conclusions

Case studies of management regimes in North America, Africa and Central America provided insights into the variability of management systems in different parts of the world while highlighting broad principles relevant to sustainable use:

❑ wildlife has value;

❑ wildlife is a public resource belonging to everyone, but government intervention is needed to conserve wildlife for future generations;

❑ use of wildlife can be controlled; and uncontrolled use of wildlife is unacceptable;

❑ wildlife populations can be perpetuated indefinitely while sustained use is occurring.

Conclusions from specific case studies that were presented included:

1. Beaver management in the north-eastern United States, dating back to the 1920s, is a model sustainable use programme that has demonstrated its long-term sustainability.

2. Waterfowl management in North America is based on the premise that conservation of the resource is the ultimate priority, use being a legitimate product of successful conservation. Key elements of the management programme include: a) strong reliance on science to guide management decisions; b) promotion of public and private sector partnerships to conserve habitat; c) harvest regimes that are cooperatively developed to promote shared benefits; and d) adaptability to changes in climate, new scientific findings and changing public perceptions.

3. In Central Africa wild game is being depleted by illegal, commercially motivated hunting that arises from the food-eating habits of the people, poverty and traditional beliefs.

4. Demonstration projects of community-based management of wildlife in Central America underscore the fact that nature conservation and improvement of the quality of life of rural people are two parts of the same process. People are the central element of sustainable development efforts. Community development, local organization consolidation and participation in decision-making are essential. An integrated approach is needed to achieve conservation and development.

Papers and Presentations

1. Introduction/Opening Comments (James Teer, Interim Chair, North America Sustainable Use Specialist Group, and Welder Wildlife Foundation, USA).

2. A Case Study in the Sustained Use of Wildlife: The Management of Beaver in the North-eastern United States (John Organ, United States Fish and Wildlife Service, USA and Gordon Batcheller, New York State Department of Environment, USA).

3. The Management and Sustainable Use of Ducks and Geese in North America (James Patterson, Consultant, Canada and Gregory Thompson, Environment Canada, Canada).

4. La chasse commerciale et la gestion durable de la faune en Afrique Central (Djoh à Ndiang, Interim Chair, Central Africa Sustainable Use Specialist Group, Ministry of Environment and Forests, Cameroon).

5. Sustainable Use of Wildlife in Central America: An Instrument for Biodiversity Conservation (Manuel Benítez, El Salvador, and Vivienne Solis, IUCN Regional Office for Meso-America, Costa Rica).

6. Seven Case Studies on Wildlife Management Carried Out by the North American Sustainable Use Specialist Group (Richard Parsons, Safari Club International, USA).

7. A Case Study of the Management of Barren-Ground Caribou from the Beverly and Qamanirjuaq Herds in Northern Canada (Kevin Lloyd, Government of the Northwest Territories, Canada).

8. Panel discussion: Kevin Lloyd (Northwest Territories, Canada), Nestor Windevoxhel (Central America), and Juan Carlos Barrera Guevera (Mexico).

1.6 Wildlife Trade and Traditional Medicine in North East Asia

Organizer: Wang Sung, IUCN Regional Councillor for East Asia

Chair: Daniel Chan, Head, Dept. of Zoology, University of Hong Kong

Rapporteur: Rhonda Schlangen

Summary

Traditional medicine has a large following throughout the world, in both East and West. Controversy about traditional Chinese medicine, or TCM, has largely arisen because some of the ingredients used are from endangered species. In particular, bear, tiger, pangolin and several types of antelope are considered to be in grave threat due to use of their parts in TCM. This workshop examined traditional medicine and its role in the life and culture of those who rely on it to use it, set forth the conservation problems related to traditional medicine use in North East Asia, and discussed what the countries of the region are doing to address the problems.

Objectives

1. To explore conservation issues relating to traditional medicine practices in the North East Asia Region.

2. To develop appropriate ways to deal with the problem of species threatened by trade in TCM.

Conclusions

Conservationists assumed that the trade in TCM would stop if 1) it was proven that [some] TCM had no effect; 2) better alternatives were provided; 3) people were educated about the sustainability problems related to TCM; and 4) trade of TCM using endangered species was banned by law. However, the reality is rather different.

❑ Many TCM have proven to be effective. For example, bear bile contains ursa diaxycolic acid, which Western doctors have tested and documented its efficacy in treating certain ailments. Furthermore, TCM has been historically proven. Users have up to 5000 years of history telling them that the medicines are effective. Suddenly showing a lab report denying the efficacy of medicines that have been used for thousands of years has little impact.

❑ Synthetic substitutes have been developed, but are not popular among users. For example, Japanese scientists synthesized and isolated bear bile. This was made into TCM with much less impact on the bear population. However, users considered the synthetic medicine to be too pure and too strong, and believed that the natural bear gall bladder was naturally buffered by the other gall bladder matter naturally occurring in the bladder in addition to the ursa diaxycolic acid.

❑ The onslaught of criticism from conservationists, particularly Western conservationists, has led some TCM users to believe that their culture is being threatened. Thus, the feeling is that TCM – and the 5000-year-old culture it represents – is what is really at risk of dying out. This perception that TCM is being attacked and needs to be protected thwarts effective conservation education.

❑ Law enforcement has worked in some cases. For example, in Taiwan, after the introduction of legislation that punished dealers for selling or carrying restricted animal products, only 6 cases were discovered in 1994 and 6 cases in 1995. No violations were found in 1996.

❑ But in some cases where governments have cracked down on wildlife trade relating to TCM, rather than curbing the trade it has driven it underground to the black market trade. Illegal trade in wildlife uses the same trafficking routes as narcotics, guns and other illegal goods.

A possible solution could be built on six factors:

❑ Respectful communication and cooperation between TCM users and conservationists. TCM users need conservation to preserve their pharmacoepia and conservationists need the cooperation of TCM users in order to be effective.

❑ When TCM goes underground, both sides lose. TCM users lose an affordable supply of medicine and conservationists have less opportunity to influence more sustainable trade.

❑ Neither conservationists nor TCM users can "win". TCM has proven it will continue at any cost. But on the other hand, current practices and rising levels of use make it unsustainable. Neither side can assume the moral high ground.

❑ All must respect cultural perspectives and background.

❑ Because wildlife is harvested by poor villagers for wealthy consumers of TCM (a wealthy Korean paid $64,000 for the gall bladder of Korea's last Asiatic Black Bear), we cannot extricate social inequality for the issue of conservation.

❑ Somehow we must find the money and political will to address this problem. The dilemma should be viewed as not East vs. West. There is a growing concern in the East among both conservationists and TCM users about the sustainability of TCM, and there is a rapidly growing number of Westerners using TCM.

Outputs and Follow-up

IUCN will continue to address the TCM issue, for example through TRAFFIC, CITES, and the Sustainable Use Initiative.

The solution should include:

❑ disseminating public information

❑ gathering information from consumers and producers about sales and purchases

❑ directing and regulating brokers, by registering illegal stocks, banning products from severely threatened species (such as rhinos), and controlling labelling

❑ raise public awareness, especially of travellers

❑ encouraging transition to alternative ingredients

❑ improving both *in situ* and *ex situ* management of target species.

Papers and Presentations

1. Nature of Traditional Medicine and Wildlife Trade with Focus on North East Asia (Judy Mills, TRAFFIC East Asia)

2. The Role of Traditional Medicine (Kuan Chung Su, Professor at China Medical College, Taichung, Taiwan and Chairman of the Committee on Chinese Medicine)

3. The Impact of Wildlife Trade for Traditional Medicine on the Region (Meng Sha, Division Director, Department of Wildlife Conservation of the Ministry of Forestry, China

4. Traditional Medicine and National Control Measures in Japan (Maki Koyama)

5. Discussion: Key Issues for Future Regional Activities (Wang Sung, IUCN Regional Councillor for East Asia.

2.1 Expanding Support to the Convention on Biological Diversity: Implementing National Biodiversity Strategies and Action Plans

Organizer: IUCN Biodiversity Programme

Chair: David Munro, Canada

Rapporteur: Caroline Martinet, IUCN

Summary

Seven presenters from various institutions (NGO, Inter-governmental, Governmental and Multilateral Development Assistance), and various perspectives (regional as well as disciplinary) discussed experience gained in the preparation and implementation of national biodiversity strategies and action plans. Nels Johnson of WRI described the lessons learned from 18 countries in the elaboration of the National Biodiversity Planning Guidelines, (WRI, IUCN, UNEP, 1995). From an African perspective, Julius Chileshe described the lessons learned in the past decade of strategy development and planning, and highlighted key issues, lessons and challenges facing strategy practitioners. Carmen Taveira discussed the role of UNEP and its support to biodiversity planning process through three projects: the preparation of Biodiversity Country Studies, Biodiversity Data Management, and National Biodiversity Strategies and Action Plans. From the perspective of the World Bank, Colin Rees described the types of assistance available for biodiversity planning and steps to mainstreaming biodiversity. Legal tools for the implementation of strategies and planning processing in Bangladesh were discussed by Mohiuddin Faroouque. Lily Rodriguez described the Peruvian experience in biodiversity planning and Stein Kollungstad of Norway presented the comprehensive approach of the government in Norway in developing a national biodiversity strategy that also integrated biodiversity into sectoral plans and programmes.

Objectives

1. To review the current status of the preparation of biodiversity strategies and action plans which have been designed by the World Resources Institute, UNEP and IUCN.

2. To promote the implementation of these strategies and plans, and identify the appropriate role for IUCN in supporting this preparation.

Conclusions

The Convention on Biological Diversity has helped governments to recognize biodiversity as national assets. The process of preparing National Biodiversity Strategies and Action Plans has assisted nations in learning more about these assets and permitted them to see how benefits from biological resources are realized, distributed and reinvested. The GEF and its three implementing agencies are supporting many countries in preparing their biodiversity strategies and action plans, and the Conference of the Parties of the Convention on Biological Diversity considers the preparation of such plans as an "enabling activity", implementing Article 6 of the CBD.

Planners should also be implementers of the strategy; the worst kind of planning is that which is farthest removed from the implementing agencies. Many planning processes have begun under pressure from external sources which has undermined plans being done in the light of self-interest or having an efficient ownership process; this has limited their effectiveness.

Biodiversity planning and strategy processes need to be linked to the nation's vision of sustainable development, as well as to local-level initiatives; such linkages can ground national strategies in reality and build momentum for their implementation. It is important to undertake a stakeholder analysis, involve all levels of society, and determine the expectations of each sector in the strategy process so as to ensure a proper balance between capacity-building, products, processes documents, and investment needs. However, strategies, plans, programmes, and policies are not legally enforceable so the necessary political will, appropriate integration into the decision-making process, and adequate resources are also needed for effective implementation. The number and options for planning and strategies are vast, and UNEP, UNDP, and the World Bank are encouraged to cooperate more effectively for greater synergy between the various major planning requirements. A diversity in approaches to national biodiversity planning will enable the needs and priorities of each country to be fully addressed.

Other key messages from the workshop:

- ❑ Biodiversity planning should have strong links to national development planning and national visions for sustainable development.
- ❑ Quality of life and biological resources are directly related.
- ❑ IUCN has an important role to play in integrating biodiversity approaches and methodologies into development activities.
- ❑ IUCN should bring a common language to biodiversity issues.

Cross-cutting issues

Given the existence of various definitions of biodiversity, educators and trainers need help in understanding biodiversity so that it can be more easily communicated at the local level. A common language is needed – the language used at the level of international meetings means nothing at the local level, and IUCN could help bring a common language to biodiversity issues.

Sufficient and operationally-effective definitions of biodiversity terms are needed in legislation. Most countries already have a sufficient legal basis and this should be a starting point for a gradual move towards change. Biodiversity conservation is a fundamental right and this can be pushed gradually. It is important to test the legal implications of ratification of the CBD (i.e., can a nation be forced to implement the Convention?). Policies, strategies and plans are not legally enforceable.

Outputs and Follow-up

❑ IUCN will use guidance from the workshop to support national efforts to prepare biodiversity strategies and action plans, on request.

❑ IUCN will continue to monitor the preparation of national biodiversity strategies and action plans, with a view to compiling lessons learned.

Papers and Presentations

1. National Biodiversity Planning: guidelines based on early experiences around the world (Nels Johnson, WRI)

2. UNEP's Support to National Biodiversity Planning (Carmen Tavera, UNEP)

3. World Bank Support for the Preparation of National Strategies and Action Plans (Colin Rees, World Bank)

4. Strategic Planning in Africa: how national biodiversity strategies and action plans fit in (Julius Mwale Chileshe, CESDC)

5. Legal Aspect of National Biodiversity Strategies and Action Plans (Mohiuddin Faroouque, Bangladesh)

6. Practical Planning for Biodiversity at the Regional Scale (Lily Rodriguez B., the Peruvian Association for Conservation)

7. Norway's Approach to Preparing its National Biodiversity Strategy (Stein Kollungstad, Ministry of Environment, Government of Norway).

2.2 The Role of GEF in Supporting the Convention on Biological Diversity

Organizer: Global Environment Facility; IUCN Biodiversity Programme

Chair: Walter Lusigi, GEF Secretariat

Rapporteur: Jose Ireneu dos Remedios Furtado, World Bank

Summary

The purpose of the workshop was to share the experiences of GEF over its first five years. The Global Environment Facility (GEF) was an innovative, inter-governmental financing mechanism for new grants and concession funds, established to exercise international responsibility for protecting the atmosphere, oceans and lakes, and biological diversity, through the collaboration of participating governments. It was established in 1990 during the negotiations on climate change and biodiversity, on a proposal by France and Germany in 1989 arising from the Brundtland Report and Montreal Report in 1987. In its 3-year Pilot Phase (1991–94), the GEF supported a wide variety of projects in different parts of the world, mainly in biodiversity. As a consequence of Agenda 21 (1992) and an independent evaluation of the GEF Pilot Phase (1993), the GEF was restructured for five years (GEF 1) beginning in 1994 to provide the interim financing for four Conventions: Convention on Biological Diversity, Framework Convention on Climate Change, Vienna Convention on Protecting the Ozone Layer, and the International Convention to Combat Desertification.

Objectives

1. To introduce the GEF and present case studies for two national projects, a regional project and a global project.

2. To promote better understanding of GEF projects and to encourage broader IUCN involvement in the preparation and submission of projects to the GEF.

Conclusions

Partnerships with NGOs. Local NGOs were involved in all projects but their sustainability was threatened sometimes by governments. They needed IUCN guidance to develop bankable projects.

Biodiversity specialists. There is a global shortage of biodiversity specialists, and hence IUCN could play a role in promoting the training of taxonomists.

Project sustainability. In some cases, project sustainability is threatened due to depletion of funds; and IUCN could assist NGOs establish and manage funds.

Health hazards. In view of emergence and re-emergence of epidemics, plagues and pest outbreaks, IUCN could promote a study exploring the links between biodiversity loss, ecological degradation and health.

Outputs and Follow-up

❏ The case studies will be published by GEF as a means of sharing lessons learned.

❏ IUCN's Biodiversity Programme and Regional and Country Offices will assist governments in designing projects for funding by GEF.

Papers and Presentations

1. National Integrated Protected Areas (NIPA) Project (Horatio Morales, Jr, Philippines)

2. Patagonian Coastal Zone Management Plan (Guillermo Harris, Argentina)

3. East African Biodiversity Project (Alan Rodgers, Kenya)

4. Introduction to the Global Biodiversity Assessment Project (Carmen Taveira, UNEP)

2.3 Restoration Ecology

Organizer: Society for Ecological Restoration

Chair: Nik Lopoukhine, Parks Canada

Rapporteur: Stephen Woodley, Canada

Summary

The workshop was very broad in scope, with presentations on the philosophy, science and application of restoration ecology. Ecosystem restoration generated considerable excitement, as both a philosophy and a practical way to remediate past human activities. Three general conclusions were evident. First, restoration ecology is redefining the art of the possible. For example, in New Zealand, rats and other predators of natural resources have been successfully eradicated from offshore islands and alien predators effectively reduced in a lowland forest, both experiments leading to significant conservation gains. Only recently, such developments were considered impossible. Second, restoration offers a philosophical message of hope, that people are part of ecosystems, rather than a plague on ecosystems. And third, these two messages combined to create a sense of excitement in the room. Restoration ecology was seen as an important focus for the IUCN.

Objectives

1. To define ways to restore degraded ecosystems to a more productive state creating a partnership among science and management.

2. To provide specific national examples of restoration ecology.

3. To discuss general principles of restoration ecology and develop recommendations for IUCN activities in the field of rehabilitation and restoration of degraded ecosystems in a wide range of different types of habitats.

Conclusions

Restoration ecology has a powerful ethical component. Ecosystem restoration was called a changing paradigm, a quiet revolution and a move toward enlightenment. Humanity and nature are seen as part of the same sphere, rather than separate entities. At its best, restoration is seen as allowing people an opportunity for personal self-transformation, community renewal and a way to "resonate with the ancient traditions of world renewal". Some have criticised restoration as a male paradigm for pushing nature around, but this was explicitly rejected by several speakers. Examples of good restoration included real participation by indigenous groups, local residents and stakeholders from a range of societal interests.

Ecological restoration was called a value, and the definition of restoration was explicitly called a value identification exercise. This gets far away from the idea of wilderness ecosystems, where humans have no impact. Ecosystems were instead seen as expressions of human value. Thus the state or condition of ecosystem is a reflection on our values.

Restoration ecology is developing as a discipline. Considerable effort was taken to discuss the origins of the restoration ecology and a definition now used by the Society for Ecological Restoration. That definition is "a process for assisting the recovery and management of ecological integrity". Ecological integrity is interpreted very broadly to include ecosystem structure and function, historical variation and regional and social context. The science behind ecosystem restoration is developing rapidly. Presentations ranged from the importance of soil processes and using thermodynamic measures of energy to assess the state of the ecosystem to assessments of the role of birds in seed dispersal. There were reports on specific restoration projects in landfill sites in New York, New Zealand lowland forest and islands, and river estuary complexes in the Netherlands. These ranged from creating new ecosystems to restoring or enhancing components of existing systems.

Other conclusions of the workshop:

❑ Restoration efforts need to be expanded to cover a wider geopolitical range of countries. Specific needs were identified for Mediterranean-type ecosystems and arid lands, specifically southern South America.

❑ Restoration efforts need to address the challenges of larger scale issues, with the specific case of large-scale desertification in North Africa being noted.

❑ A systematic, worldwide status assessment of species and communities that are most in need of restoration should include a categorization of those species and communities that would most benefit, what are the chances of success and what are likely costs. This was seen as triage approach to classifying restoration needs.

Outputs and Follow-up

❑ Individuals from the IUCN family were encouraged to join the Society for Ecological Restoration, with a notice of a major symposium on restoration of tropical ecosystems in 1997.

❑ IUCN's Commission on Ecosystem Management will consider establishing a task force on restoration ecology, seeking methods to restore lost or damaged ecosystem functions.

Papers and Presentations

1. Introduction: The Objectives of Introducing Ecological Restoration as a Fundamental Component of Ecosystem Management Applicable Throughout the World (Nik Lopoukhine, Parks Canada)

2. Elements of Ecological Restoration (E. Higgs, University of Alberta)

3. Ecological Restoration Strategies (S. Handel, Rutgers University)

4. Rebuilding Ecological Processes (Jim Harris, University of London)

5. Man-made Nature in a Man-made Environment: The Ijsselmonding Project on Habitat Restoration (Robert Verheule, The Netherlands)

6. Island and "Mainland Island" Restoration: The New Zealand Experience (William Mansfield, Director General, New Zealand Department of Conservation)

7. Ecological Restoration: An Immediate Conservation Paradigm (Bill Jordan, Editor, *Restoration and Management Notes*).

2.4 The Contribution of Science to Ecoystem Management

Organizers: Edward Maltby, IUCN Commission on Ecosystem Management (CEM); Martin Holdgate, United Kingdom

Chair: Christopher Hails, WWF-International

Rapporteur: Hillary Masundire, University of Botswana

Summary

In seeking to provide the best possible advice to the global community, IUCN draws heavily on the science of ecology. The Commission on Ecosystem Management is seeking to find better ways to apply science to management at the ecosystem scale. This will involve encouraging scientists to make their work more relevant to real-life problems, and managers to define their problems in ways that enable the former to make an optimal contribution. The challenges are very great, since ecosystem function and dynamics remains a matter of important scientific enquiry, and because of the constantly changing demands made by humans for goods and services from ecosystems. This workshop will build on the findings of the First Sibthorp Seminar held in London in June 1996 to produce principles for integrated management of natural resources, based on approaches at the ecosystem level.

Objectives

1. To articulate principles for integrated management and ecosystem-based conservation and resource utilization.

2. To publish examples and analysis of lessons learned (positive and negative).

3. To plan future action to develop guidelines to implement and promote these principles.

4. To contribute to the development of the CEM strategy document and work plan for 1997–1999.

Conclusions

Major Questions

The Workshop addressed some fundamental questions. Perhaps the biggest is whether the ecosystem approach is really valid for conservation management. A second linked question is whether the same principles can be applied to management on land and in the sea. The third big question is what we really mean by management. The fact is that we manage human actions that in turn have an impact on ecosystems. We use the status of key, prominent or valued species as indicators of the state of an ecosystem and we judge the "success" or "failure" of our efforts by their responses. We do not monitor or manage ecosystems as a whole.

The Principles of Ecosystem Management

The draft principles developed at the Sibthorp Seminar constitute a useful starting point, but they clearly need adaptation to more specific national and local conditions, especially because management at the local scale is critical. They may need subdivision, because not all are equally important in all situations, while at some local scales, sub-sets of a principle may be highly relevant. Several of the principles are discussed further below.

Principle 1. Ecosystems must be managed in a social context. There was a broad consensus of agreement of this principle, which involves management by a process of adjustment of human impacts. There must be a management plan to articulate social choices. But good communication is needed to secure social consensus for proposed actions. Moreover, we must allow for the fact that the social context is changing continually, and opportunistic responses are necessary. The social context must not be too narrowly defined, and local societies are subject to many major external influences.

Principle 2. Ecosystem integrity is different from ecosystem health. It must be remembered that ecosystem integrity is different from ecosystem health and sustained productivity. We need to maintain diversity and resilience as a basis for alternative futures. The workshop saw this demonstration in relation both to steppes and wetlands.

Principle 3. Management is the art of the possible, at the scientific as well as the social level. Science can provide guidelines, highlight areas of uncertainty, and identify possible mistakes to avoid. But the spatial scale of management needs to be chosen with sensitivity to the dynamics of the system itself, and to the scales of movement of component species, including migrants. On land, protected areas, safeguarded by buffer zones and habitats and linked by corridors, can be defined relatively exactly and their management will need to have very different spatial dimensions. Both boundaries and management prescriptions will be less capable of relationship to specific geographical features. Managers should always proceed with caution.

Principle 4. Change is inevitable. But we need to define alternative scenarios with care, recognizing that a single change may allow several social choices. Options must be kept open, but clear pathways must be signposted NO ENTRY.

Challenges for the Commission on Ecosystem Management

Invasive species. The inevitability of species invasions, as biogeographical barriers are broken down, should be noted. Efforts to prevent invasions need to be judged against a sharp test of practicability – and the implications of unavoidable invasions for ecosystem management need to be assessed.

A multi-disciplinary approach. Interdisciplinary action can confer "hybrid vigour" on the resulting management practices. It is essential that the CEM creates a forum for multi-disciplinary communication among experts from different backgrounds, including biologists, economists, social scientists and those from the humanities.

Scientific principles. The CEM should seek the further development of the topics discussed in the workshop. However, cross-linkages must be established with other Commissions, to which these concepts are also highly relevant. Building on the former Commission on Ecology, CEM should become a basic scientific powerhouse for IUCN.

Provision of guidance. The CEM should provide IUCN with guidance on the Union's inputs to external bodies like the Convention on Biological Diversity, the Framework Convention on Climate Change, the Convention to Combat Desertification and Drought, and the Intergovernmental Panel on Forests. Furthermore, the workshop urged the CEM to produce operational guidelines for ecosystem managers. Such guidelines must be written in simple, easy-to-understand language appropriate for the target audience. CEM was also urged to popularise the science of ecosystem management.

Outputs and Follow-up

❑ Publication of the First Sibthorp Seminar Papers (Title: *The Scientific Basis of Ecosystem Management for the Third Millennium*).

❑ A CEM Steering Committee meeting to prepare the Commission's workplan.

Papers and Presentations

1. Introduction to workshop (Hans Lundberg, CEM)

2. How to Underpin Ecosystem Management: The findings of the Sibthorp Seminar (Martin Holdgate, UK)

3. Ecosystem Management in Terrestrial and Wetland Environments: The challenge for CEM (Edward Maltby, Royal Holloway Institute for Environmental Research)

4. Ecosystem Management in Marine Environments: The challenge for CEM (Tundi Agardy, WWF-US)

5. Putting Theory into Practice (Gerardo Budowski, CATIE, Costa Rica)

6. Summary (Martin Holdgate, UK).

2.5 Biological Diversity Knowledge and Monitoring: Inventory and Database Methodologies adapted to the needs of Sustainable Development

Organizers: IUCN National Committee of France; IUCN National Committee of Canada

Chairs: Robert Guilbot, Secretary-General, Office for Eco-Entomological Information, France; Leopold Gaudreau, Director of Conservation and Natural Heritage, Ministry of Environment and Wildlife, Quebec, Canada

Rapporteur: Patrick Blandin

Summary

Biodiversity conservation is an essential condition for sustainable development. Biodiversity modifies itself naturally, but the increase of human impacts involve general degradation risks. The implementation of conservation politics, and the restoration of damaged ecosystems are ways to counterbalance this negative tendency. In order to estimate the efficiency of conservation activities, it is necessary to follow the evolution of biological diversity at the local, national and international levels. While conservation databases which enable information to be mobilized to guide management area critically important, significant methodological problems still exist. Databases show a wide diversity of approaches depending on countries and organisms, illustrating the importance of compatibility of data.

Concerning data utilization, the problem is to focus on satisfactory scientific aggregation methods to respond to the different needs of the users, taking into account if they are local, national or international. Regarding the rapidity of on-the-ground changes, the necessity of rapid procedures has been highlighted. Finally, the importance of a clear ethic regarding the property and the use of scientific data appeared to be a major condition to ensure the sustainable mobilization of data management networks

Objective

To discuss how biodiversity databases can meet the needs of sustainable development.

Conclusions

Action to conserve biological diversity should take into account: i) the level of organizations considered: species, communities, ecosystems, landscapes, and ecological regions; and ii) the level of decisions considered (local, national or international).

The objective is generally to emphasize the dynamic trends (regression, progression, stability) of species (quantitative and spatial variations) and ecological systems (variation of components and/or size) by distinguishing the spontaneous and anthropogenic factors that influence these dynamics.

To be efficient, follow-up should be based on an accurate typology of the reference state of the ecological systems adapted to the various levels of organization (ecological regions, landscapes, ecosystems, communities, etc.).

The standardization of data registration methods is essential to ensure data comparability in space and time. It implies a strict definition of the descriptors related to each level of organization. These descriptors have also to be defined following the most efficient registration on-the-ground.

At all stages – from the incorporation of data into the languages and data aggregation processes for national and international synthesis – scientific validation procedures have to be implemented.

IUCN, based on its Members' experiences, should contribute to the progressive harmonization of methodologies concerning: i) the typology of ecological systems; ii) the definition of state references; iii) the standardization procedures of the collection and data management; and iv) scientific validation procedures. IUCN would then be able to contribute to the harmonization of databases, avoiding expensive redundancy and emphasizing the formation of a global information network on biodiversity.

Outputs and Follow-up

IUCN will create, in collaboration with Members, a Biodiversity Conservation Information System.

Papers and Presentations

1. Introduction by the Chair (Robert Guilbot)

2. Information on the organisation and interaction of the major international agencies (World Conservation Monitoring Centre, Cambridge)

3. Managing information on Nature in Europe (Dominique Richard, Centre Thématique Européen)

4. National Heritage Centres: an International Perspective (The Nature Conservancy, USA)

5. EUROMAB (J. Lecomte, President MAB Committee for France)

6. Ecological Mapping of Natural Regions (J.P. Ducruc and V. Gerardin, Direction of Conservation and Ecological Heritage of the Ministry of Environment, Quebec).

2.6 Dealing with Alien Invasive Species

Organizer: IUCN Invasive Species Specialist Group (SSC)

Chairs: Ian Macdonald, WWF-South Africa; Gerry Lee, Canadian Wildlife Service

Rapporteur: John Cooper

Summary

The problem of invasive species was highlighted in a number of talks which gave examples from various parts of the world. Examples given in terrestrial and aquatic habitats were shown to reflect serious problems, which, however, were not always insoluble, although prevention (not allowing introductions) was always better than cure (attempting control and eradication programmes after introductions). Draft IUCN guidelines for the prevention of biodiversity loss due to biological invasion were tabled and described and an appeal made for comments and additions to be sent to the ISSG chair before their final adoption in early 1997.

Objectives

1. To call for the prevention of the introduction of alien species which threaten ecosystems, habitats or species.

2. To identify ways and means to enhance the IUCN/Species Survival Commission Invasive Species Specialist Group, in order to encourage a more vigorous response to the problem of invasive species.

3. To describe the dimensions of the problem and specify how IUCN can best contribute to the growing international response to this critical issue.

Conclusions

The threats to biodiversity posed by alien invasive species are given insufficient attention. Awareness of the risks to biodiversity and ecosystems caused by alien invasive species need to be heightened both within and outside the IUCN community. Within IUCN this could be achieved by approaching the Commissions, programmes and task groups to identify the alien species problems within their sphere of expertise. For example, all specialist groups of the Species Survival Commission should be asked to identify invasive species problems and consider what actions were required. This information should then be fed back to the Invasive Species Specialist Group for synthesis and suggested actions. It was agreed to submit a resolution to this World Conservation Congress requesting that IUCN address the issues of invasive aliens in all its forums.

Animal welfare groups may be doing harm to biodiversity by protecting introduced species. Concern was expressed that animal welfare groups had taken up the cause of protecting introduced species in a number of countries. NGOs which are dependent on public support are particularly vulnerable to this type of pressure. This is likely to be an increasing problem that needs to be addressed by negotiation and education. Governments need to set guidelines and to enact regulations in this regard.

The world needs a database on information about alien invasive species. It was proposed to hold a workshop to develop a *modus operandi* for producing an invasive species database, and an offer was made to hold such a meeting in May 1997 in Canada. Such a database should aim to be predictive, in allowing judgements to be made on the likelihood of alien species becoming invasive in different ecosystems.

Governments need to assign clear responsibility for invasive species issues. Governments need to reassess how decisions are made when treating potentially and actual invasive species. Currently, "non-environmental" ministries, such as agriculture and health, often make decisions which do not always take into account the nature-conservation risks associated with the introduction of alien plants and animals.

Cross-cutting issues

This workshop covered gender-neutral issues. In terms of communication it was agreed that a certain level of sensationalism was sometimes desirable to heighten awareness among the public and the media. Governments need a single set of legislation and one legal authority to handle alien issues within countries. The role of law is particularly important in the prevention of new introductions. Such prevention was found to be by far the most cost-effective approach to solving alien problem. In certain circumstances, such as the North American Great Lakes ecosystem, it is the only effective way of limiting the problem. Often, the legal implications are international in scope, especially where ecosystems occur across national boundaries.

Outputs and Follow-up

❑ Publication of agreed IUCN Guidelines for the Prevention of Biodiversity Loss Due to Species Invasions

❑ IUCN will participate in the international project to prepare a global strategy for alien invasive species. This participation will include SSC's Invasive Species Specialist Group, the Environmental Law Centre, and the Biodiversity Programme

❑ SSC's ISSG will carry out an active programme to deal with invasive species

❑ A workshop on producing an invasive species database will be held in Canada in May 1997.

Papers and Presentations

1. The Global Significance of Alien Invasions for Nature Conservation (Jeff Waage, Director of the Imperial Institute of Biological Control, UK)

2. Conspicuous Consumption, Commerce and Alien Species (Val Geist, University of Alberta, Canada)

3. Global Strategy for Alien Invasive Species (Hal Mooney, ICSU/SCOPE and Stanford University, USA)

4. Presentation of the IUCN Draft Guidelines on the Management of Alien Invasives (Mick Clout, Chair, SSC Invasive Species Specialist Group)

5. Alien Plant Control: Anatomy of a Public Partnership (Gerry Lee, Canadian Wildlife Service)

6. Exotic Species in the Great Lakes: Problems, Solutions and Outstanding Issues (Allan Dextrase, Canada)

7. Databases of Invasive Alien Species: Local to Global Initiatives (Ian Efford and Erich Haber)

8. Invasive Species Control: A Canadian Perspective on the Road to Recovery (Gerry Lee).

9. IUCN's Response to the Problem of Alien Invasive Species (Jeffrey A. McNeely, IUCN Chief Scientist).

2.7 The Bioregional Approach in Practice

Organizer: World Resources Institute (WRI)

Chair: Kenton Miller, WRI

Rapporteur: Nels Johnson, WRI

Summary

Science and experience are demonstrating that protected area strategies to conserve bio-diversity are an insufficient response to dynamic changes in landscapes, advancing agricultural frontiers, pollution, and climate change. The challenge is to plan and implement conservation programmes at geographical scales that make sense ecologically, economically and socially. This workshop examined the conceptual basis for bioregional approaches to conserving biodiversity, and practical experiences from the United States, Colombia, and Pakistan and closed with a discussion on lessons for planning and implementing bioregional management and how IUCN can promote bioregional approaches for managing biodiversity. The workshop touched on many of the key ideas discussed at other WCC workshop sessions including: Cooperative Management; Corridors; Man and the Biosphere Programme; Ecosystem Management; and Restoration Ecology.

Objectives

1. To summarize the conceptual and practical basis for using bioregional approaches to conserve biodiversity.

2. To illustrate, through case studies, how cooperation among governments, communities, NGOs and corporations is being used to protect, restore and sustainably use biodiversity at a landscape or bioregional scale.

3. To identify lessons, based on recent experience, that could form the basis for developing initial guidelines to assist conservationists, researchers, and natural resource managers to plan and implement effective bioregional management strategies.

Conclusions

Bioregional management is a cooperative, adaptive process to sustainably manage and conserve biological resources at a regional scale. Bioregional management approaches typically involve stakeholder-led cooperative efforts to protect, restore, and sustainably use biological resources at a regional scale. Bioregional management goals usually include biodiversity conservation, sustainable economic development, and the protection of vital ecosystem processes. Adaptive management processes to monitor, evaluate, and readjust planning and management activities on the basis of new information and learning are an important feature of effective bioregional management efforts. The rubric of "bioregional management" draws upon a number of different approaches, including bioregionalism, biosphere reserves, integrated conservation and development projects, and the rapidly expanding body of ecosystem management efforts in the United States and elsewhere. Each builds upon a strong ethic of "place" and stewardship.

Bioregional management approaches share a strong ethic of "place" and include activities across the landscape. The concept of "place" is central to bioregional management efforts for scientific, economic, and social/cultural reasons. Species, genetic variability, the processes and functions that make up ecosystems, and the natural and human disturbances that maintain a dynamic environment all occur in a particular geographic space. So too, economic activities and human social interactions are centered or anchored in geography. Together, biological, economic, and social processes on the landscape help to define a bioregion. Scaled to relevant ecological processes, economic activities, and community dynamics, bioregional management approaches are place-based efforts often defined by a problem of common concern (for example, the restoration of a nearly extinct wild salmon population). Typically, the scope of bioregional management efforts includes activities across the entire surrounding land and seascape including – in the case of salmon restoration – wildlands, farms, commercial forests, urban areas and infrastructure, fishing zones, riparian corridors, and the high seas. These activities will cross ownership, political, and sometimes international boundaries.

The success of bioregional programs depends upon establishing a voluntary partnership of those groups, organizations, individuals and corporations who have a stake in the future of the region. A stakeholder is potentially any individual or group who is already there, with rights of access and ownership (recognized under modern legal or traditional tenurial regimes). The point is, whoever is on the land or the waters and whoever is employing the place for whatever purpose must be part of the conservation program if measures are to be taken to achieve biodiversity objectives. Stakeholders who do not become full partners in planning and implementing programs can end up hindering the program's chances of success. So planners and policy-makers should get to know the stakeholders, their concerns, interests and perspectives, and should seek ways to involve them in the planning and implementation process. One key is to help them select issues of common interest for action and investment. These individuals and groups may need help gaining access and skills to participate fully in the decision-making process, and all stakeholders need access to key information as well as a fair distribution of benefits. Clear and shared goals are essential for the long-term success of a voluntary partnership.

Leadership and trust are indispensable to successful bioregional efforts. Whether in Pakistan, Colombia or the United States, leadership by an individual or a small handful of people has been at the root of successful bioregional conservation efforts. Effective local leadership may be the most important and yet least tangible factor in developing a successful regional conservation effort. Organizations based outside the region with an interest in promoting bioregional approaches should be prepared to seek out and work with local leaders from the earliest stages of project development. A lengthy process to build trust between different groups (especially between local and "outside" groups) may be required. For example, BirdLife International was able to work effectively to conserve key habitats in the Palas valley of Pakistan only after they gained the trust and cooperation of local communities by working with them to improve health services and education in the region. In the United States, The Nature Conservancy has generated local support for zoning and development planning that protects the Virginia Barrier Islands Reserve by establishing itself as a committed member of the community that works to catalyze sustainable economic development and improve social conditions. A long-term commitment to have a local presence and to work with others on solutions to regional problems that go beyond environmental concerns helps to establish the trust needed to find solutions to biodiversity conservation problems.

Bioregional management efforts must be based on the best available science and continually adapt to new information and knowledge. Perhaps the most promising feature of bioregional management is its experimental nature. The ability to adapt to changing local, national, and international realities, as well as the recognition of scientific, political, economic, and cultural uncertainties is a key element of bioregional management projects. In addition, adaptively managing a bioregional project implies communication with local players as well as providing appropriate information so that those managing local resources are well informed about the consequences of their actions. Since most bioregional projects are new, few policies are in place which support the establishment of such efforts. Thus, those involved in bioregional projects have had to be innovative in establishing mechanisms that collect, monitor, and evaluate information appropriate to the goals and objectives of the bioregional management effort. Even more challenging is to develop a process that effectively incorporates new information and knowledge into planning, decision making, and management activities in the field.

Outputs and Follow-up

❑ WRI is working with IUCN and other organizations to develop a "bioregional management" module for the BIOCAP program – a cooperative effort to provide training materials and workshops on key issues related to the implementation of the Convention on Biological Diversity.

❑ WRI will work closely with the organizers of the WCPA experts meeting in Albany, Australia in November 1997 to develop a vision statement on the challenges that protected areas must meet in the 21st century. Central to this vision is how protected areas fit into a broader bioregional-context and how the tools and strategies of bioregional approaches must become those of protected area managers.

❑ The IUCN/World Commission on Protected Areas and WRI are collaborating in the development of case studies on bioregional management approaches for the design and management of mountain conservation corridors.

Papers and Presentations

1. Bioregional Management: Implementing Biodiversity Goals in Practice (Kenton Miller, Nels Johnson, and Marta Miranda, WRI)

2. The Challenges of Building Constituency for Bioregional Management Among Residents and Resource Users in a Complex Social and Cultural Region : The Case of the Sierra Nevada de Santa Marta, Colombia (Juan Mayr Maldonado, Fundacion Pro-Sierra Nevada de Santa Marta, Colombia)

3. Managing Larger Landscapes with Local Residents: Cases from The Nature Conservancy's Experience (Bruce Runnalls, The Nature Conservancy, USA)

4. Applying Ecosystem Management on Public and Private Lands: Lessons Learned from the Keystone Dialogue on Ecosystem Management in the USA (Todd Barker, Keystone Center).

3.1 Caring for the Earth: 25 Years of World Heritage Action

Organizers: UNESCO World Heritage Centre

Chairs: Walter Lusigi, Christina Cameron, Rob Milne, Hal Eidsvik

Rapporteur: Pedro Rosabal, IUCN

Summary

The World Heritage Convention provides an international framework for action to protect the world's special places. World Heritage Sites face many challenges in the face of industrial development and agricultural encroachment. The World Heritage Convention must adapt to changing circumstances and promote a new vision for the future of the world's natural heritage. This workshop proposed a practical agenda for the successful implementation of the Convention.

Objectives

1. To raise the awareness of opportunities and challenges presented by the World Heritage Convention.

2. To review strategies and past recommendations for the implementation of the Convention, to assist in formulating an IUCN strategy which will be presented to the World Heritage Committee.

3. To provide a forum for the presentation of case studies, public discussion and the development of recommendations as well as the refinement of a World Heritage resolution to the IUCN WCC.

Cconclusions

World Heritage is a bridge to the future. World Heritage Sites are a source of pride, wonder and inspiration and are a "gift to the world" held in trust by this generation for future generations. World Heritage provides a unique opportunity to foster environmental awareness at all levels, particularly for the young. Innovative education programs focused on World Heritage, such as the UNESCO World Heritage Youth Forum, need to be encouraged and expanded.

Partnerships are needed. Achieving the goals of the World Heritage Convention requires partnership. Established partnerships, such as those between the UNESCO World Heritage Centre and IUCN, are crucial; these need to be consolidated and expanded. New partnerships are also required, at all levels. At the international level, this could involve enhanced partnerships with other Conventions, particularly the Convention on Biological Diversity. At national levels, better partnerships are required between agencies that manage World Heritage Sites and other relevant organizations and agencies. Opportunities for transboundary World Heritage Sites between two or more countries need to be explored, and expanded in the case of existing areas, such as the Victoria Falls Site between Zambia and Zimbabwe. Exchange schemes between countries which aim to improve World Heritage Site management, such as those between Indonesia and New Zealand in relation to the Udjung Kulon World Heritage Site, need to be developed. At local levels better and more effective working relationships with local people need to be established. Planning for World Heritage Sites needs to be considered in the context of regional land use and innovative planning schemes, such as the Bow Valley Study in Canada's Banff National Park, need to be implemented.

Resources need to be mobilized. A number of World Heritage Sites are under pressure. Targeted financial assistance is required. A number of sites have been placed on the "World Heritage in Danger" list; such listing should be seen as a positive measure which can trigger efforts, at all levels, to address the pressures faced. Opportunities such as those provided by the Global Environmental Facility need to be explored.

The management of World Heritage Sites needs to be strengthened. Management of World Heritage Sites needs to be strengthened. Focused training programs need to be developed to enhance the skills of World Heritage managers. The prestige of "World Heritage" must be instrumental in raising the stature and esteem of protected area managers in society. Stronger and more effective institutions need to be developed. Every use needs to be made of modern technology to strengthen communication and dialogue between World Heritage Site managers, including through the use of the Internet and strengthened information management networks such as the WCMC World Heritage Information Network. Guidelines to assist the management of World Heritage Sites need to be developed but these need to be practically focused.

Cross-cutting issues

The management of World Heritage Sites must involve key groups from local communities. The role of women in this process is critical, particularly in relation to communication of the values of World Heritage in a way which makes sense to local communities. More effective communication is particularly important in relation to World Heritage. This is applicable at many levels. At the *international* level there is a particular need for better communication and interaction with other Conventions, particularly the Convention on Biological Diversity. At the *national* level, communication with key policy and decision makers is needed to ensure that World Heritage is clearly understood. In many cases there is not a clear understanding of World Heritage, and why it is important, and this in turn has often caused problems. At the *local* level there needs to be communication of how World Heritage is relevant to local communities, with particular emphasis on the many positive benefits associated with World Heritage. Specific legislation is also needed at a national level, as in Australia, to ensure that the Convention is translated in a way that is relevant to the unique needs and circumstances of each country. Such legislation needs to be responsive to changing circumstances.

Outputs and Follow-up

❑ An educational slide programme setting out the goals, objectives and structure of the Convention. The slide programme is intended for use in other meetings and workshops;

❑ Publication of the proceedings and recommendations;

❑ A special edition of the World Heritage newsletter on Natural World Heritage Sites;

❑ Guidance to IUCN on how to integrate the World Heritage Convention more fully in its work.

Papers and Presentations

1. Introducing World Heritage (David Hales, USA)

2. World Heritage Strategy: A View from the World Heritage Centre (Bernd von Droste, World Heritage Centre, Paris)

3. The Natural World: A slide presentation (Jim Thorsell, IUCN)

4. Enhancing Implementation of the Convention (P.H.C. Lucas, CNPPA Natural Heritage)

5. World Heritage in Southeast Asia (N. Ishwaran, World Heritage Centre, Paris)

6. Galapagos: Under Threat but Not in Danger (Michael Blimsreider)

7. Yellowstone in Danger: An NGO Perspective (Mike Clark, USA)

8. The Biodiversity Convention and World Heritage (Jeff McNeely, IUCN)

9. Cross Frontier Planning, Zambia/Zimbabwe (N. Nalumino/Peter-John Meynell)

10. Canadian Rocky Mountains (Donna Petrochenko, Canada)

11. Funding the Flagships (Ken Hornback)

12. World Heritage Convention and IUCN (Jay Hair, IUCN President).

3.2 Managing Protected Areas in a Changing Climate

Organizer: Adam Markham, WWF

Chairs: Claude Martin, WWF-International; Peter Bridgewater

Rapporteur: Pedro Rosabal, IUCN

Summary

Global warming presents a major threat to the management of many protected areas. Impacts of this warming will include altered weather patterns, changes in timing and distribution of precipitation, some changes in extreme events such as heavy rains and droughts, and sea level rise. This workshop assessed the potential threat of climate change to protected area networks and discussed management strategies to minimize ecosystem perturbations.

Objectives

1. To identify state of the art knowledge in relation to climate change threats to species and ecosystems.

2. To discuss practical adaptation strategies which can be developed for ecosystems where climate change impacts will have particularly significant impacts.

Conclusions

Climate change has major implications for protected areas. All presentations highlighted the major impacts of climate change on the establishment and management of protected areas, and the interrelationship with social and economic issues. These impacts are equally important for marine and terrestrial protected areas. They include: a) potential species extinction and displacement; b) accelerated introduction of invasive species; c) degradation of marine and other ecosystems; and d) discontinuity in ecological processes. These impacts have potentially grave implications for the future management of protected areas and for biodiversity conservation in general. Some 50% of protected areas are projected to undergo significant changes in vegetation type over the next 100 years, according to climate models. Enormous changes are already taking place in relation to many national parks, as highlighted in the presentation to the workshop on the Rocky Mountains National Park.

Awareness of the impacts of climate change needs to be increased. The large amount of information on climate change and its specific environmental impacts indicates very disturbing trends in relation to the impacts of climate change on protected areas. However, this message is often not getting through to key target audiences. This is a serious failing that must be addressed. Information relating to impacts must be clearly presented, with an emphasis on drawing out practical implications and priority actions, appropriate to the target audience. For example, information directed at protected area managers must focus on practical implications for the ways in which protected areas need to be established and managed. A particular emphasis should be placed on influencing decision makers and this will require clear and understandable messages that highlight policy implications.

Better dialogue and coordination between relevant parties are required. Climate change scientists and protected area managers rarely talk to each other and more forums which encourage such dialogue, such as this workshop, need to be initiated. Considerable comparable research work is underway in relation to protected areas and climate change. For example, Parks Canada has established a research programme on this subject and a case study was presented on the impacts of climate change on a number of protected areas in the United States. Clearly there is a need to establish linkages between similar studies such as these. At the *international* level, closer interaction is needed between the Climate Change Convention and the Convention on Biological Diversity. This could include aspects such as: a) establishing formal and informal contacts between members of the respective secretariats of each Convention; b) attempting to achieve greater conservation input to IPCC meetings (the workshop noted that recent IPCC reports have limited coverage of the impacts of climate change on biodiversity); c) the development of protocols to either Convention which relate to climate change and biodiversity; d) a statement of principles relating to climate change and conservation, with a particular emphasis on protected areas (this could in effect provide a basis for soft law in much the same way as the Statement of Forest Principles); e) closer interaction at national levels between respective country delegations to the COP meetings of both conventions. At the *national* level closer cooperation is needed between agencies working in fields related to climate change and protected areas, as well as between scientists and protected area managers. Within IUCN, the potential for cooperation between the Commissions, particularly CNPPA and CEL, was noted in relation to this topic. Such efforts should be closely linked with those of the WWF Climate Change programme.

Climate change may provide a catalyst for rethinking approaches to protected areas. Climate change implies change, at the species, ecosystem and biota level. Traditional protected areas have focused on specific delineated areas and they thus may not be responsive to climate change effects. Protected areas have static boundaries and it is necessary to plan beyond their boundaries, to address the challenges of climate change. Protected area establishment and management must be proactive and adapt to changing circumstances. Specifically, protected areas need to be complemented by other conservation efforts such as the establishment of conservation easements and riparian conservation zones. Increased use also needs to be made of approaches such as: a) bioregional planning; b) biosphere reserves; c) IUCN protected area categories V and VI; and d) landscape ecology. Such approaches must be linked to a strengthening of the management of existing protected areas; ecosystems which are stressed are less able to cope with the impacts of climate change. Protected area managers and government agencies also need to plan on broader temporal (e.g. hundreds of years) and spatial (e.g. 1,000 sq. km) scales in relation to climate change. This represents a radical shift from current approaches which tend to be much more narrowly focused in time and space. Climate change considerations may also require that the future designations of protected areas anticipate species and ecosystem distribution under different climate change scenarios.

Cross-cutting issues

The impact of climate change will be most apparent where women are primarily engaged in natural resource management in and adjacent to protected areas. The need for more effective communication was raised at numerous stages during the workshop and some specific issues are identified above. The key need is for better and more targeted information, to target audiences at different levels, which will change attitudes and approaches in relation to climate change and protected areas. CNPPA and WWF could play an important role in this area. The potential interaction between the conventions on Climate Change and Biodiversity is outlined above. The following additional points were noted: a) the need for greater interaction between the Climate Change Convention and other international conventions, such as Ramsar, CITES and the Convention on Migratory Species; and b) the respective secretariats should work closer together on the common cross-cutting issues and develop further instruments or protocols to address the effect of climate change on biodiversity and protected areas. At a national level, many issues are relevant to climate change and protected areas, such as planning, EIA, pollution, economics (particularly incentives and disincentives), and natural resource management. Appropriate legal instruments should be developed. Ecologists, protected area managers, planners and others should work more closely with environmental lawyers to ensure that effective measures are introduced and enforced at international, national, and local levels. Linkages between CNPPA and the Commission on Environmental Law should be encouraged in relation to this issue. The preparation of a joint CNPPA-CEL study on the topic of climate change and protected areas was suggested. Such activities need to be supplemented by appropriate training in environmental law, aimed particularly at protected area managers, but generally also at relevant decision makers.

Outputs and Follow-up

❏   A practical guidelines document which identifies key issues and response strategies relating to the issues of climate change and protected areas;

❏   Provision of a forum for interaction between climate change scientists and conservation managers to discuss this issue.

Papers and Presentations

1. Protected Area Managers and Management in the Face of Climate Change (Peter Bridgewater, Biodiversity Group, Environment Australia)

2. Marine Protected Areas : An Extended Outlook (Tundi Agardy, WWF-US)

3. Modelling Climate Threats to Ecosystems and Developing Adaptation Strategies (Patrick Halpin, Duke University, USA

4. Global Change and the Northern Rockies (Thomas Stohlgren, United States Geological Survey)

5. Ecosystem Resilience, Biodiversity and Climate Change: Setting Limits (Jay Malcolm, University of Toronto, Canada)

6. Climate Change and Freshwater Ecosystems (Connie Hunt, WWF-US)

7. Localizing Global Climate Change Impacts: Vulnerability Analyses of Selected Protected Areas in the US (Janine Bloomfield, Environmental Defense Fund, US)

8. Forest Conservation and Joint Implementation: The Example of Belize (Joy Grant, The Nature Conservancy Programme, Belize)

9. Potential Impacts of Climate Change on Protected Areas in East Europe and parts of the former USSR (Alexander Kozhanikov, Centre for Biodiversity Conservation, Russia).

3.3 Biosphere Reserves: Myth or Reality?

Organizers: Peter Bridgewater, Chairman, International Coordinating Council of the MAB Programme, Pierre Lasserre, UNESCO-MAB

Chairs: Bruce Amos Canada; Rokhaya Fall, Senegal; Dean Bibles, US-MAB; Peter Bridgewater, Australia

Rapporteurs: Sami Mankoto, Jane Robertson, UNESCO-MAB

Summary

In the early 1970s, UNESCO pioneered an alternative approach to nature conservation based on the principles of ecosystem representativeness, participation of local people, ensuring a scientific and educational base and promoting international cooperation through networking. Today, the biosphere reserve concept is hailed as being "more than a protected area". This workshop explored the reality of putting the biosphere reserve concept into practice and demonstrated the challenges and the rewards of such a multifunctional approach.

Objectives

1. To discuss the relevance of the World Network of Biosphere Reserves for the implementation of the Convention on Biological Diversity.

2. To share the experience of people actively working in biosphere reserves representing different interests such as nature conservation, socio-economic benefits from protected areas, scientific research and monitoring , electronic communications networks, and local government.

3. To explore what is meant by "local participation".

Conclusions

Biosphere Reserves is a concept whose time has come. Biosphere reserves were considered ahead of their time when they were first developed in the early 1970s. Their time has now come. Biosphere Reserves, with their interrelated objectives of conservation, development and logistic support, offer a practical and creative approach to the imperative of linking conservation and sustainable development. This model is likely to become increasingly important, for both developed and developing countries, as we move into the next century and as demands for the use of scarce natural resources accelerate. However, there is a need to ensure that the potential of the Biosphere Reserve model is fully achieved and the Seville Strategy for Biosphere Reserves, which stemmed from the 1995 International Biosphere Reserve Conference in Seville, Spain, is an important step in this direction.

This Strategy sets out a clear and concise vision for Biosphere Reserves in the 21st century and identifies the objectives and activities necessary to achieve this vision. It was noted that the flexibility of the Biosphere Reserve concept accommodates much recent thinking in relation to conservation, particularly in relation to the shift from a cadastral approach to a bioregional approach in relation to protected areas, and the IUCN revised system of protected area classification. While each Biosphere Reserve will be defined in accordance with local conditions, it was stressed that all Biosphere Reserves should fulfil an appropriate balance between their three basic functions, including participation in the scientific programmes within the World Network.

Partnerships are needed. Achieving the goals of the Biosphere Reserves requires partnership. Established partnerships, such as those between the UNESCO Man and the Biosphere Programme and IUCN, are crucial; these need to be consolidated and expanded, on the basis of mutual interest and support. A number of practical suggestions for achieving this were suggested, in relation to the IUCN Commission on National Parks and Protected Areas (CNPPA), including the appointment of a Vice-Chair for Biosphere Reserves. New partnerships are also required, at all levels. At the *international* level, this should involve enhanced partnerships with certain Conventions, particularly the Convention on Biological Diversity. The clear link between Article 8 of this Convention and the Biosphere Reserves was noted but this linkage has yet to be fully utilized. Cooperation between international donor organizations and national organizations is also required to mobilize resources to assist the development and more effective management of Biosphere Reserves. At *national* levels, better partnerships are required between agencies, organizations and individuals involved in the establishment and management of Biosphere Reserves. This is particularly pertinent to Biosphere Reserves as there are often many different jurisdictions and interest groups involved. Clear and effective coordination mechanisms are required. At the national level there is also scope for developing transboundary Biosphere Reserves between two or more countries and the practical application of this was outlined at the workshop in relation to a Biosphere Reserve shared between a number of countries in Central Europe, notably the Eastern Carpathians. At *local* levels better and more effective working relationships between Biosphere Reserves and local people need to be established. At this level, Biosphere Reserves also offer suitable opportunities for experimenting pilot actions in sustainable development of water, energy, agro-forestry, aquaculture, etc. in a synergistic manner.

Local people have to be more involved. Many of workshop presentations and interventions from the floor stressed the need for more effective involvement of local people in the establishment and management of Biosphere Reserves. It was noted that the Biosphere Reserve model has this as a principal tenet but that this is not always achieved at the field level, for a variety of reasons. Three key factors of success for the more effective involvement of local people in Biosphere Reserves: (a) the need to demonstrate direct benefits associated with the Biosphere Reserve, such as was outlined to the workshop in relation to the Mananara Nord Biosphere Reserve in Madagascar; (b) the need for the agency responsible for management of the Biosphere Reserve, especially the core area, to have an outward focus and for this to be linked with a targeted communications/outreach strategy; and (c) the need for local people to have a real, rather than token, input to decisions concerning the Biosphere Reserve. Local communities have considerable knowledge which can be usefully applied to improve the management of Biosphere Reserves.

Communications using the World Network of Biosphere Reserves needs to be strengthened. The development of appropriate networks is particularly important and will become increasingly more so. The example of UNESCO/MABNet and its related networks (EUROMABNet and MABNet-Americas), which are information management networks linking a number of Biosphere Reserves around the world, was presented to the workshop and it was agreed that this is an extremely useful model. The potential for electronic communication through the Internet was also emphasized. It was noted that information must cover socio-economic as well as biological data and that the collection and use of information should be coordinated between key actors to the greatest extent possible. Training is also required for biosphere reserve coordinators in a range of areas, including information management. This latter topic was illustrated by the presentation on the CI/UNTEL/UNESCO project under which a number of training workshops are being organized in different parts of the world.

Cross-cutting issues

The management of Biosphere Reserves must involve key groups from local communities. The role of women in this process is critical, particularly in relation to communication of the values of Biosphere Reserves in a way which makes sense to local communities. More effective communication is particularly important in relation to Biosphere Reserves. This is applicable at many levels. At the *international* level there is a particular need for better communication and interaction with other Conventions particularly the Convention on Biological Diversity. At the *national* level, there is a need for communication with key policy and decision makers to ensure that Biosphere Reserve concepts are clearly understood and also that they are built into national biodiversity strategies. At the local level there needs to be communication of how Biosphere Reserves are relevant to local communities, with particular emphasis on the many positive benefits associated with such reserves. The World Network of Biosphere Reserves is governed by the Statutory Framework for Biosphere Reserves which sets out a definition, selection criteria, a designation procedure and a periodic review of all biosphere reserves. At the national level, Biosphere Reserves provide a framework to integrate conservation and approaches to sustainable development. This involves the use of national legislation at hand. In some cases however, countries such as Mexico have enacted specific national legislation for Biosphere Reserves. Due to the inherent need for Biosphere Reserves to be responsive to changes – whether ecological or social – such legislation needs to be flexible.

Outputs and Follow-up

Publication of presentations and synthesis of discussions indicating progress achieved in implementing the results of the International Conference on Biosphere Reserves (Seville, 1995).

Papers and Presentations

1. The Reality of the World Network of Biosphere Reserves: Its Relevance for the Implementation of the Convention on Biological Diversity (Peter Bridgewater, Australia, Chair of MAB International Coordinating Council)

2. Biosphere Reserves and Protected Areas: What's the Difference? (Adrian Phillips, Chair, CNPPA/IUCN)

3. Across the Frontiers : Biosphere Reserves in Bioregional Management of Shared Ecosystems in Central Europe (Zusana Guziova, Slovakia)

4. Biosphere Reserves are Good for Nature : Viewpoint of a Conservationist (Carlos Ponce, Peru)

5. Networking Using Biosphere Reserves (Rodger Soles, US MAB National Committee and Brian Block, Coordinator MABNetAmericas)

6. Can Biosphere Reserves be Truly Multifunctional? A Case in Canada (Charles Roberge, Réserve de biosphère de Charlevoix, Quebec)

7. The Economic Reality of Local Community Participation in Biosphere Reserves: A Case in Madagascar (Raymond Rakotnindrina, Madagascar)

8. Biosphere Reserves: The Views of a People's Representative (Christobal Triay Umbert, President of the Council of the Menorca Biosphere Reserve, Spain)

9. Biosphere Reserves: Their Potential to Monitor Forest Biodiversity (Francisco Dallmeier, Smithsonian Institution, USA)

10. Strengthening Biosphere Reserves (Sean Gordon, Conservation International, USA)

11. A major challenge to the Seville Strategy: Do People Really Participate in Biosphere Reserves? A discussion with the participation of Mohamed Ribi (Morocco), Dean Bibles (MAB-US), Rokaya Fall (STAP & MAB Senegal), Bettina Laville (France), Juan Antonio Menendez-Pidal (MAB-Spain), Jurgen Nauber (MAB-Germany), Javier Garcia (Argentina).

3.4 Stewardship: Promoting Conservation and Sustainable Use on Private Lands

Organizers: Jessica Brown and Brent Mitchell, Quebec-Labrador Foundation, Atlantic Center for the Environment

Chairs: Jessica Brown and Adrian Phillips, UK

Rapporteur: Pedro Rosabal, IUCN

Summary

In the face of declining public resources for land acquisition, management and enforcement of protected areas, new options for land conservation and sustainable use need to be explored. The stewardship approach – which encourages individual and community responsibility for sound natural resource management – offers a means to expand conservation beyond protected areas. The workshop reviewed the experience on the application of the concept and contributed to an assessment of best conservation practice on private lands.

Objectives

1. To examine the application of stewardship to natural and heritage area management, with particular emphasis on the application of this concept beyond the boundaries of formal protected areas.

2. To highlight how conservation professionals are relying on stewardship techniques to address key conservation challenges.

3. To investigate the potential application of stewardship models to alternative institutional options for protected areas management.

4. To explore the potential of stewardship to enhance management of protected areas, particularly IUCN categories V and VI.

Conclusions

Stewardship is the way of the future. Traditional models of protected area management, involving management of such areas by government agencies, are changing. It is increasingly clear that a broader view and new approaches are required. This is the fundamental tenet of stewardship, which is defined as: ***efforts to create, nurture and enable responsibility in landowners and resource users to manage and protect land and natural resources***. Stewardship involves a range of approaches including: (a) conservation easements; (b) lease arrangements; (c) subsidies; (d) covenants over land; and (e) agreements between local communities and management agencies. Two important principles underly stewardship: first, that it is based on effective partnerships and cooperation between relevant stakeholders, particularly local communities, land owners and relevant government agencies; and second, that it is supported by relevant and effective education/communication programmes.

Stewardship is an international concept. Examples were presented from around the world in relation to stewardship. In the South Pacific the innovative South Pacific Biodiversity Conservation Program is spearheading the development of conservation areas on traditionally-owned land in complete partnership with traditional owners. Experience from the United States and New Zealand illustrated the effective use of conservation easements and management agreements in achieving conservation objectives on private land in full consultation with private and indigenous land owners. Experience from Tanzania, Peru, Brazil, Poland, and India indicates that programmes which encourage greater participation of local people and non-governmental organizations in conservation are taking root. A wide range of approaches fit under the umbrella of stewardship and no one model will apply in all circumstances. Approaches must be tailored to the unique circumstances of each country.

What makes Stewardship work? Key Factors of Success. What makes stewardship work or fail? Key factors of success that are essential if stewardship is to work include: (a) a climate for productive partnership between relevant stakeholders; (b) ideally, a legal framework which is tailored to the unique circumstances of each country; (c) participation by all interest groups; and (d) adequate resources. Stewardship is also enhanced by sharing experience and information; this workshop fulfilled a valuable role in this regard.

The rangers are no longer afraid of going into the villages. This was the message passed on by Lota Melamari, the Director General of the Tanzanian National Parks Agency (TANAPA). He noted the shift of emphasis in the management in relation to national parks and other protected areas in Tanzania: the original focus was for management of species and ecosystems within the national park system, with limited focus on the involvement of local communities living in and around such areas. This focus is now changing and the management of protected areas now places emphasis on working with and not against local communities and particularly on examining ways in which local communities can benefit from activities associated with protected areas, such as hunting. This shift has changed the way in which local communities view staff within the park agency – from an original role as an enforcer to a role as a partner. Thus, the rangers are not afraid of going into the villages any more. Similar experiences were also raised in relation to India where an ecodevelopment programme is being developed which aims to encourage local development initiatives in association with protected areas.

Partnerships are essential – between local communities, government, non-governmental organizations, and the private sector. Stewardship requires strong and effective partnership between key stakeholders. Local landowners must be involved and can play a leadership role. As noted by John Cook from The Nature Conservancy, conservation of species and ecosystems requires the leadership and involvement of local people. He further noted that the effective involvement of people requires security of land tenure for future and traditional uses more than subsidies or financial grants. The increasing involvement of the private sector in the establishment and management of protected areas was noted and a presentation from the World Conservation Monitoring Centre (Michael Green) noted that there are an increasing number of privately run protected areas in Eastern and Southern Africa. Approximately 7% of the land area of the Republic of South Africa is now under private protection, slightly more than is managed under the government system of protected areas. The involvement of the private sector appears to be an increasingly apparent trend in many parts of the world. The important role of the non-government sector was highlighted in a presentation from Peru (Gustavo Suarez de Freitas) where it was noted that a Peruvian NGO has played a major role in the establishment and management of protected areas. This example also highlighted that such involvement should be in full partnership with relevant government agencies and illustrated how such partnerships can broaden traditional approaches to protected areas management; in the case of Peru, to place greater emphasis on the involvement of people and to encourage the use of a broader range of protected area categories. A similar experience is underway in Brazil promoted by IBAMA to enhance conservation of biodiversity on private land.

Cross-cutting issues

Women have an important role to play in relation to the implementation of stewardship programmes within local communities; they are a key target audience. Good communication is essential if stewardship programmes are going to be successful. Such communication must ensure that the right message is delivered at the right level: targeting of the audience and the message is essential. Stewardship programmes need a strong legislative and institutional base. It is critical that legislation is tailored to the specific circumstances in each country. Legislation can apply at many levels – for example, local regulations may be most effective in relation to the most effective implementation of local zoning schemes or easement arrangements. Traditional and customary law may also be most appropriate in certain situations, such as in the South Pacific.

Outputs and Follow-up

❏ Publication of the proceedings and recommendations.

❏ Guidance on how to expand the application of this concept especially due to its potential value to the implementation of the Convention on Biological Diversity.

Papers and Presentations

1. Stewardship: A Working Definition (Brent Mitchell, Director of Stewardship Programmes, QLF/Atlantic Centre for the Environment, US)

2. Protecting Landscapes: Global and Local Stewardship (P.H.C. Lucas, Vice-Chair CNPPA/World Heritage, New Zealand, and Michael Beresford, Director, International Centre for Protected Landscapes, UK)

3. Nature, Culture and Stewardship: Reinterpreting Conservation at the New Marsh-Billings National Park (Nora Mitchell, Olmsted Centre for Protected Landscapes, National Park Service, US)

4. Lessons from 12 years of NGO-Government Co-operation in Protected Areas Management in Peru (Gustavo Suarez de Freitas, Director, Pro Naturaleza, Peru)

5. Wildlife Management Areas: A New Approach to Involving Rural Communities (Lota Melamari, Director, Tanzania National Parks, Tanzania)

6. Conservation by Design: The Nature Conservancy Framework for Mission Success (John Cook, Vice President, The Nature Conservancy, US)

7. A Survey of Private Conservation Initiatives in Eastern and Southern Africa (Michael Green, World Conservation Monitoring Centre, UK)

8. Stewardship in Central Europe (Rafal Serafin, Environmental Partnership for Central Europe)

9. A System of Private Reserves to Protect Brazil's Natural Heritage (Sonia Wiedmann, Director, Private Reserves Programme, IBAMA, Brazil)

10. The Ecodevelopment Strategy in India (Kishore Rao, Deputy Inspector General (Wildlife) Ministry of Environment and Forests, India).

4.1　Marine and Coastal Conservation

Organizers:　S. Olsen, G. Kelleher, M. Williams, J. Waugh, L. Kimball, P. Holthus

Chairs:　Plenary Sessions: T. Agardy, E. Gomez

Concurrent Theme Working Group Sessions:
　　S. Olsen, G. Kelleher, M. Williams, L. Kimball

Rapporteurs:　L. McManus-Talue, R. Salm, C. Nauen, L. Kimball, P. Holthus

Summary

IUCN is addressing many marine and coastal issues and has the potential to play a critical, catalytic role of leadership and coordination on these issues. The goal of IUCN efforts should be the conservation of marine biodiversity and the sustainable use of marine and coastal resources. This report includes working group sessions on integrated coastal management, marine protected areas, fisheries, and international marine law and policy. Integrated Coastal Management (ICM) and Marine Protected Areas (MPAs) are important means for IUCN to work to achieve this. IUCN's efforts should be integrated with appropriate international law and policy instruments. A key resource focus should be fisheries and the ecosystems which support them, especially for high diversity ecosystems and areas with a high dependence on fisheries (e.g., small islands).

Objectives

1. To present and review the state-of-the art in marine and coastal conservation and sustainable development issues.

2. To discuss and develop the directions, priorities and role of IUCN in addressing these issues, especially in the context of the Union-wide Marine and Coastal Programme.

Conclusions

Marine Law and Policy

IUCN's role in marine law and policy should include efforts to develop "integrated convention management and information resources" in order for parties to be able to understand the relationship among conventions and how they respond to, and relate to, ecosystem and bioregional scales, including by developing regional approaches to link conventions and the relevant ecosystems. This could also include assisting states and international organizations in understanding multiple convention obligations and their relationships based on a matrix of state obligations and putting in place a strategy for using the conventions to achieve specific goals, and promote better internal coordination among states in preparing for the many convention fora.

IUCN should develop a focused international review of oceans issues that concentrates on determining priorities, setting policy directions, and coordinating among international policy and programme developments within IUCN. The work of IUCN should build on IUCN expertise in species and protected areas/habitats and tackle broader aspects of the land/sea interface, with a specific focus on linking back to sources of impacts on marine species and ecosystems and the sectors where the impacts originate. We must improve diagnostic tools and technical practices related to marine resources uses (e.g., fisheries) and impacts on the marine environment (e.g. land-based activities) and integrate these tools into management approaches (e.g., marine and coastal protected areas). Overall major actors and agencies need to be educated on the above issues at all levels.

Fisheries

Fisheries ecosystem management is emerging as a new paradigm for fisheries management, embodying the precautionary approach. Fisheries science and management need to be linked with ecosystem management to develop the new paradigm of fisheries ecosystem management, especially to understand the linkages between fishing and the ecosystem which supports the fish. IUCN should continue to work on the process for evaluating marine fish species for the Red List, with particular attention to refining the criteria and involving more fisheries experts in the process. IUCN efforts should focus on small scale fisheries, especially in areas where fish are a critical part of livelihood and a high percentage of nutritional needs, e.g., on small islands, and focus on the human dimension, especially human resource development and the involvement of all stakeholders.

The use of market forces in fisheries management may be an effective tool in influencing at least some aspects of fisheries; for example, reducing subsidies is an important market tool for reducing fishing pressure. However, market measures might lead to major social and economic costs to control fisheries in some communities. Efforts to develop the certification of products from sustainable fisheries should be continued and IUCN may have a role in helping to determine criteria for certification. However, care must be taken in developing the certification of fisheries, as an effective certification process would likely lead to a greater economic concentration within fisheries, at the expense of small, independent, community-based fisheries.

Integrated Coastal Management

An ICM learning process needs to be developed, particularly by developing methodology and indicators for measuring success in a variety of settings and scales, with case studies as a basis for drawing out the lessons. Measuring ICM with appropriate indicators can be used to document post-implementation impacts and build financial sustainability into project design. The application of the lessons into a learning culture will provide important input in moving on to the "how" of ICM, e.g., how to build ownership/participatory approaches and how to build useful and effective networks.

Linkages are needed within key sectors (e.g., tourism, mariculture and fisheries) to develop economic incentives for ICM and for the private sector to be more involved in ICM. At the government level, policy should call for ICM as an instrument or strategy and for training in ICM at all appropriate levels. Overall, we must enhance ICM development at a regional level through collaboration and build networks of ICM managers as well as scientists, via IUCN commissions as appropriate.

Marine Protected Areas

Reconciling biodiversity conservation with community needs, particularly economic needs, is critical because when there are clear economic benefits to the greatest number of stakeholders, getting MPAs established will be easiest. Economic benefits are of major interest at local level particularly in subsistence cultures and for stakeholders with direct economic dependence on resources (notably fishermen). We thus need to bring benefits from MPAs to communities, while still addressing biodiversity conservation objectives by developing mechanisms to achieve community participation in conservation and MPAs that benefit the community directly. Outreach programmes involving awareness activities and workshops targeting both the antagonists and proponents of MPAs are an essential component of this.

IUCN efforts towards MPA development should involve all stakeholders, whether supportive or antagonistic, and use the greatest possible array of arguments and incentives to ensure involvement in the MPA process, identifying common areas of interest. We must recognize the need to develop appropriate approaches on a case by case basis, and use the appropriate mix of direct actions and inducements as each case requires, with both participatory (bottom-up) and directed (top-down) efforts in the appropriate combination. MPA development must incorporate the role of MPAs as a powerful catalyst for, and a vital component of, Integrated Coastal Management and as important in supporting fisheries and other industries. IUCN work on implementation of the Global Representative System of MPAs should continue, with attention to the biogeographic classification basis for this, and effort at assisting the establishment of national and regional MPA systems.

Outputs and Follow-up

❏   The deliberations, conclusions and recommendations of the Marine and Coastal Workshop will provide guidance to the IUCN in identifying the appropriate directions, priorities, strategies, role and actions to address marine and coastal issues.

❏   A proceedings of the Marine and Coastal Workshop will be compiled to include the Keynote and Issues Papers, a summary of Theme Working Group discussions and the conclusions and recommendations.

Papers and Presentations

Plenary Keynote Papers:

1.   Increasing the Efficiency of Integrated Coastal Management Initiatives (S. Olsen)

2.   A Global Representative System of Marine Protected Areas (G. Kelleher)

3.   Conservation and Fisheries: Roadmap for the New Era (Williams)

4.   International Marine Law and Policy (T. Scully)

Plenary Presentations by Representatives of International Organizations:

5. UNESCO IOC (C. Morry)

6. UNEP (I. Dight)

7. UNDP (P. Reynolds)

8. World Bank (C. Rees)

Theme Working Group Session Papers:

9. Financing integrated coastal management in Latin America and the Caribbean: Directions for a new strategy at the Inter-American Development Bank (M. Lemay)

10. Making ICM a Sustainable Process in the Philippines: Hindsights for Future Directions (L. McManus-Talue)

11. Restructuring Coastal Planning and Management in Developing Countries (E. Perez)

12. MPA Problems and Solutions in East Africa (R. Salm)

13. MPA Problems and Solutions in South America with Particular Reference to Local Community Management of Marine Protected Areas (S. Campello, G. Georgiadis)

14. MPA Problems and Solutions for the South Pacific and Small Island States (D. Stewart)

15. MPA Problems and Solutions for the High Seas (M. McCloskey)

16. The Role of MPA's in Sustainable Fisheries and Maintenance of Biodiversity (P. Auster)

17. The Role of Marine Protected Areas in Sustainable Fisheries (J. Sobel)

18. The Roles of Community Based Fisheries Management and MPAs in Coastal Fisheries (A. Alcala)

19. The Concept of Fisheries Ecosystem Management – Current Approaches and Future Research Needs (M. Sissenwine)

20. Future Challenges for Fisheries Resource Assessment in the Aid of Fisheries Management (J. Rice)

21. New Approaches to Development Cooperation in Capture and Culture Fisheries (C. Nauen)

22. Coastal Fisheries and Marine Development Issues for Small Islands (T. Adams)

23. Influencing Fisheries Conservation: An International NGO Perspective (M. Sutton)

24. The Possibility of International Law and Institutional Arrangements for Sustainable Use of Marine and Coastal Biodiversity (Lee Kimball).

4.2 Enhancing Biodiversity Conservation in Arid Lands

Organizers: Abdulaziz H. Abuzinada (Director, National Commission for Wildlife Conservation and Development, Saudi Arabia) and Moustapha Soumaré (United Nations Development Programme Office for Drought and Desertification – UNSO)

Chairs: Abdulaziz Abuzinada, Moustapha Soumaré

Rapporteurs: Eugene Joubert (NCWCD), Hillary Masundire (University of Botswana)

Summary

This workshop on biodiversity conservation in arid lands reviewed the latest understanding in dryland degradation. Principles for the successful definition and implementation of sustainable development projects in countries affected by desertification were proposed, and subsequently included in Resolution 1.56: Combating Desertification. This resolution calls for a greater involvement of the IUCN constituency, and the international donor community, in the action programmes to combat land degradation under the Desertification Convention.

Objectives

1. To discuss new approaches for arid land management with a view to providing guidance to IUCN members, commissions and programmes on how best to enhance arid land biodiversity.

2. To discuss how new financial resources could be made available to combat desertification.

3. To produce a resolution calling for an increased involvement of the IUCN constituency in arid land management and desertification issues, in cooperation with all interested experts, governments, international institutions and aid agencies.

Conclusions

Arid lands constitute about 47% of the world's land area and support about 25% of the world population. The distinction between aridity and desertification was clearly identified: aridity is not the cause of desertification. Desertification and the degradation of biodiversity in arid lands result from poor agricultural practices and management regimes combined with economic factors linked to efforts to increase productivity. Loss of biodiversity is only one of several consequences of desertification. The spread and impact of desertification is more pronounced in arid lands. Poverty is an important issue; many populations live in these arid lands with no other resources at their disposal to meet increasing lifestyle expectations. Not enough is done to tackle the issue of poverty in arid land communities.

Participatory approach to arid land management

Biodiversity conservation has shifted, or must shift, from species protection to ecosystem management and restoration. As biodiversity is the main source of livelihood for inhabitants of most arid lands, resource management must take place within a socio-economic context. There is need for more scientific knowledge to enable informed interventions to reverse negative trends in biodiversity conservation. Indigenous communities in arid lands have a wealth of knowledge gained over long periods of living in these ecosystems. Such knowledge should not be ignored in formulating research projects and "modern" management systems.

Sustainable use of natural resources is a more efficient tool for conservation of biodiversity than their strict protection. Projects and programmes must be designed in cooperation with the local communities concerned, taking into account traditional knowledge systems. Local communities must be closely involved in the implementation of activities, since participation at the grass-root level is absolutely essential for the success of any project or programme.

However, while local communities are expected to take responsibility for project and/or programme formulation and implementation, they most often do not have the legal status to take on those responsibilities. For example, local communities may be required to properly manage wildlife resources (if game ranching has been chosen as a viable management option) or grazing lands which are legally owned by the State. Therefore, mechanisms for local community empowerment, including granting of access rights to natural resources, must be clearly defined and officially recognised in the national legislation or in its by-laws. Furthermore, a return to traditional arid land management practices should be carefully considered.

At the same time, alternative forms of livelihoods that reduce land degradation and loss of biodiversity should be developed. These include (i) eco-tourism, (ii) game ranching, (iii) sustainable use of medicinal plants and (iv) use of non-timber forestry products. New sustainable grazing systems must be developed in order to reduce or reverse arid land degradation.

International programmes and instruments

The Global Environmental Facility (GEF) has allocated US$160 million to fund efforts to improve the conservation of biodiversity in arid lands in 1997–2000. GEF will fund projects and programmes that fit into three of its focal areas: biodiversity, climate change and international waters. Such projects or programmes should aim to improve (i) land-use planning, (ii) farming systems, (iii) community forestry management and (iv) watershed management. The Convention to Combat Desertification encourages functional cross-linkages with other conventions, such as the Conventions on Biological Diversity, Climate Change, Ramsar, and institutions such as GEF, FAO and others, in order to effectively reverse current desertification trends. Contracting Parties to these conventions are urged to formulate new initiatives to combat desertification, emphasizing the need for action plans at national, sub-regional and regional and, ultimately, global levels. The Desertification Convention also emphasises the need to create an enabling environment in order for the action plans to be developed and implemented effectively in drylands, the Convention to Combat Desertification can constitute a powerful tool for biodiversity management.

The need to raise and spread awareness on issues of desertification was emphasised. Such awareness is necessary at all levels from grassroots to the highest national and international institutions.

Likewise, there is also need to inform people about the existence, objectives and mandates of the various conventions that relate to biodiversity conservation in arid land.

Cross-cutting issues

Women are generally left out of the decision-making processes even though it is recognised that women play a significant role in natural resource use in arid lands. Women often have to grapple with the effects of decisions in which they had no involvement; to reverse this trend, policies, programmes and projects should take into account the role of women in arid land management and restoration.

Outputs and Follow-up

❑ IUCN members, commissions and programmes will seek to become more involved in dryland ecosystem management, including socio-economic and cultural issues related to desertification.

❑ IUCN will assist with the definition of strategies for the international donor community, in which a greater emphasis will be given to programmes and project activities related to desertification. These strategies must be area- and problem- specific (as opposed to generic), locally applicable and, ideally, should incorporate a process by which responsibility for management is transferred to local communities. Furthermore, they should be designed to meet the livelihood needs of those who are affected by management activities.

❑ IUCN will consider a survey to evaluate ongoing projects relating to the various issues of arid land biodiversity and economics, with a view to summarising knowledge on traditional management systems and to providing guidance on strategic research topics relating to biodiversity conservation in arid lands.

❑ IUCN will assist its members to understand the linkages between conventions, and related bi- and multi-lateral institutions, so that members can derive benefit from these initiatives.

Papers and Presentations

1. Biodiversity in drylands: challenges for sustainable policy development (Samuel Nyambi, UNSO)

2. New approaches for arid land management: a comparative analysis of successful methodologies (Franklin Cardy, Elizabeth Migongo-Bake and Robert Muggah, UNEP)

3. The value of dryland biodiversity (Anthony Imevbore, Obafani Awolowo University, Nigeria)

4. Restoration of desert ecosystems through wildlife management: the Saudi Arabian experience (Abdulaziz Abuzinada, NCWCD)

5. Arid lands and the Global Environment Facility (Walter Lusigi, GEF)

6. The Desertification Convention and linkages with other Conventions (Robert Ryan, Convention to Combat Desertification).

4.3 Linking Mountain Protected Areas to Create Large Conservation Corridors

Organizer: Lawrence S. Hamilton, Vice-Chair (Mountains) CNPPA (Now WCPA)/IUCN

Chairs: Lawrence S. Hamilton, Egbert Pelinck, James Thorsell, Hemanta Mishra

Rapporteur: Linda S. Hamilton

Summary

This workshop laid out the conceptual basis for bioregional mountain corridors, presented some methodologies for achieving linkages, and promoted a vision of global-scale corridors such as the Andean Cordillera, or even an inter-hemispheric "Conservation Corridor of the Americas". Case studies of initiatives in this direction were presented for the Apennines, Karakorams, Southern Appalachians, Andes, Australian Great Dividing Range, Rocky Mountains, Cascades, Central America and the mountains of Alaska/Yukon. Strategies for their realization were discussed by the various presenters. Small working groups met to discuss: methodology; marshalling public support; bioregional concepts and options; and achieving conservation controls in the linkage areas.

Objectives

1. To bring to the WCC a vision and strategy to surmount the problems of the relatively small size and fragmented nature of mountain protected areas, if biodiversity is to be conserved and especially in view of climate change impacts.

2. To demonstrate that mountain ranges offer some of the best remaining opportunities for linkages that can accommodate bioregional planning for both nature conservation and sustainability of nature-friendly human uses of land.

3. To bring together individuals who have been planning and implementing some of these large mountain conservation corridors to exchange ideas and reinforce commitment.

4. To present to attendees, and subsequently in publications and exhibits, an inspiring view of these initiatives from around the world, so that others might be stimulated.

Conclusions

The need

Because of the rapid rate of fragmentation of natural ecosystems, scientific and environmental citizenry concern about the viability of these isolated systems and their biodiversity has been growing. Many scattered initiatives have arisen focused on providing connectivity and linkages for the diurnal or seasonal movement of wildlife. Most of these have been at a local or landscape level within states or nations, involving such devices as hedgerows, tunnels under roads, riparian corridors, underpasses, and "stepping stone" patches of wildland or wetlands. Prime examples are the "Econet" system which has been developed for the Netherlands, and the sheep-driving road reserve re-vegetation for threatened marsupials in Victoria and Western Australia.

For some time now there has been a similar concern that many if not most national parks and other protected areas are too small in themselves to maintain their rich heritage of biodiversity. This has led to efforts to incorporate protected areas into a regional context with buffer zones and other extensions which focus on conservation in landscapes under human use. Mountain parks must also include a full range of altitudinal zonation, not just summits. This is particularly important as climate changes.

Recently a vision has arisen in a few places for maintenance or restoration of large bioregional corridors in which existing national parks and protected areas in mountain ranges are linked to provide gene flow and biodiversity conservation for all biota. Such large corridors may embrace significant parts of, or even entire, mountain ranges. They often cross state or national borders and involve transborder cooperation in management. They are particularly important for species migration in the event of climate change. They are of great significance for the wide-ranging large carnivores such as wolf, bear, lynx, and others.

While riparian river corridors of conservation are urgently needed and of great importance, the mountains of the world provide the last best chance for protecting wildlands, and connecting them with conservation area linkages to form large, linear bioregions. These would involve all IUCN categories of protected areas in an integrated whole.

At the same time, concern has been growing among landowners, local governments and planners, that the fragmented, piecemeal approaches to land use planning is not providing suitable and sustainable results. The dwindling *per capita* supply of high-quality water for domestic use, irrigation, industry and recreation is forcing people to look at headwaters on a much larger, bioregional scale, in "nested" catchments. Other water problems, such as floods and sediment control, have long been recognized as only susceptible to management on a large watershed or basin wide level. The need for achieving true sustainability in mountain farming or in forestry, and at the same time plugging in where appropriate, such other land uses as mining and tourism, also pushes us toward planning large bioregions, in which protected areas of various kinds have a key role.

Melding the approaches

These two approaches come together when we expand the planning horizon to a large bioregional scale in mountain areas. Which approach leads the way in initiating action will depend on the regional situation. Where there are still large areas of wildland with few permanent human inhabitants, as in the Northern Rocky Mountains, the enlargement (altitudinally as well as longitudinally) of existing parks (perhaps with peripheral or buffer zones) and the connection of these units along the mountain spine by conservation corridors is the way to proceed. Where the mountain landscapes are in various intensities of human use, as in the European Alps, innovative extensions of existing regional nature parks and national parks (which include people) along with conservation corridors of nature-friendly human use can achieve the desired result. In both cases, whether or not it is mainly "government land" involved, local inhabitants (in or near the area) and distant users of the area both need to be fully involved in the planning and decisions.

Some recent initiatives

Around the world various initiatives have arisen to promote the dream of large bioregional mountain corridors of connected protected areas. One of the farthest advanced is the Mesoamerican Biotic Corridor extending through the seven countries of this mountainous isthmus. It is supported by a treaty of October 1994 in an "Alliance for Sustainable Development". In the northern Rocky Mountains a Yellowstone-to-Yukon protected area corridor has been conceived, and is almost a reality. In New South Wales the 1996 declaration of a new 90,000 ha South-East Forests National Park has closed the gap to create a continuous corridor along Australia's Great Escarpment of 150 km of public land, with a potential for an additional 450 km being considered by the NSW government. An altitudinal corridor from the tropical Manas Tiger Reserve in India to the 4,900 m peaks of Black Mountain National Park in Bhutan has just been created by an addition to the Royal Manas National Park in Bhutan. Bolivia and Peru created in 1995–96 two new parks which provide a 9.3 million ha transborder Andean slope corridor.

The potential worldwide is very real. A glance at a map of protected areas of all kinds in the Southern arc of the European Alps shows tremendous possibilities for such a corridor of 250 km extending north from Alpi Maritime (Italy) and Mercantour (France), two parks already operating with a high degree of cooperation and exchange. Look at the Tatras, Austrian Alps, Altai, Pamirs, Karakorams, Atlas and see the vision. The Mountain Theme of IUCN's World Commission on Protected Areas has grasped this dream, and is actively seeking support for individuals, organizations and governments who have dared to share this dream.

Outputs and Follow-up

❏ A poster display of 12 mountain corridor initiatives was exhibited at the World Conservation Congress in the Exhibit Hall. A somewhat modified version of this exhibit will be displayed at The George Wright Society Conference on Making Protection Work – Parks and Reserves in a Crowded, Changing World, in Albuquerque, New Mexico, 17–21 March 1997.

❏ An article on Mountain Conservation Corridors has been prepared for the State of the World's Mountains Policy Document for the Special UN Session in June 1997 (Rio plus Five).

❏ An article will be prepared for the Fall 1997 issue of the journal *Wild Earth*.

❏ A collaborative effort has been initiated with World Resources Institute for including concepts and these workshop case studies in a WRI publication on Bioregional Planning.

❏ A publisher will be sought for the 3 concept papers and 10 case study presentations, as a proceedings of the workshop.

❏ The Mountain Theme of the World Commission on Protected Areas will actively support these initiatives and promote new ones as a major thrust of its programme. Potentially this will influence other IUCN programmes.

Papers and Presentations

Concepts

1. Introduction and Rationale for Workshop (Lawrence Hamilton, CNPPA/IUCN)

2. 21st Century Vision – A Conservation Corridor of the Americas (and Beyond?) (James Thorsell, World Heritage/IUCN)

3. A Concept for Bioregional Planning and Issues in Implementation (Kenton Miller, World Resources Institute)

4. Conservation Biology Approaches to Large Protected Bioregions (Steve Gatewood, The Wildlands Project)

5. A Method for Identifying and Assessing Corridors that Link Protected Areas (Margaret Carr, University of Florida, USA)

Current projects

6. Southern Appalachians Wild Corridor Project (Tom Hatley and Hugh Irwin, Southern Appalachian Forest Coalition, USA)

7. Southern Great Dividing Range Protected Area Corridor (Graeme Worboys, National Parks and Wildlife Service, Australia)

8. The Karakoram Constellation of Protected Areas (Stephan Fuller, IUCN Pakistan)

9. Apennines Green Range (Franco Tassi, Il Centro Parqui, Italy)

10. Andean Spectacled Bear Habitat Corridor for Venezuela and Beyond (Edgard Yerena, SSC/IUCN, Venezuela)

11. A Tropical Andean Protected Area Corridor (Bolivia-Peru) (Roderic Mast and Carlos Ponce, Conservation International, Peru)

12. A Meso-American Biological Corridor (Paseo Pantera) (Mario Boza, Comision Centro Americano para Ambiente y Desarrollo, Costa Rica (Archie Carr III and Jim Barborak, Wildlife Conservation Society, USA)

13. Yellowstone to Yukon Biodiversity Strategy (Harvey Locke, Canadian Parks and Wildlife Association; and The Wildlands Project

14. A Protected Bioregion in Yukon/Alaska (Scott Slocombe, Wilfrid Laurier University, Canada)

15. International Cascades National Park Proposal (Phil Voorhees, National Parks and Conservation Association, USA)

Synthesis of small working group sessions

16. Methodology for Identifying Linkage Corridors (Margaret Carr and Hugh Irwin)

17. Public Support and Coalitions (Steve Gatewood and Phil Voorhees)

18. What Are Feasible Incentives for Private Land Use in the Linkage Areas? (Carlos Ponce and Archie Carr III)

19. Bioregional Concepts and Options (Graeme Worboys and Scott Slocombe).

5.1 Communication: The Key to Successful Strategies

Organizers: IUCN Commission on Education and Communication

Chair: Yolanda Kakabadse, Director Futuro Latinamericano, Ecuador and CEC

Rapporteur: Dhunmai Cowasjee, IUCN Pakistan

Summary

People are the problem for environmental policy and the solution. To mobilise people to take ownership and responsibility, communication needs to be an integral part of the government policy cycle. It needs to be used along with other instruments. Yet it is often forgotten, or poorly used, resulting in costly mistakes. Nonetheless, "cost-saving" cuts usually target communication. The context for communication is changing. Communicators have to find different ways of communicating and cooperating with the public. The motto for good communication is think (plan) before you act; and do not jump to means (e.g., brochures, mass media) before you know what you are trying to do. In the end education and communication turns policy making into a participatory process that can lead to a change in behaviour for the environment.

Objectives

1. To increase understanding of the role of communication in strategies for sustainability.

2. To identify success factors for international agencies, governments and NGOs to manage communication and education as an integral part of strategies of all types.

3. To provide input for follow-up action by CEC.

Conclusions

The problem: The scientific perception. Conservationists often neglect communication, perhaps believing that scientific facts speak for themselves. Among the scientific community this might work, but other people perceive the world in different ways, which is their reality. This perception of reality is coloured by emotional as well as intellectual reactions. The only reality is that of the target group. Environmental communication is the art and science of connecting with how a target group perceives the environment. Communication depends on listening, to understand the people's realities. Based on this, communication provides information in ways that build on attitudes, knowledge and values and contributes to setting up processes that can lead to individual and social changes for sustainable development.

The context for communication. We are in an Information Society, where environment must compete for attention in a 500-channel world. People still consider environmental problems important, but in western countries feel that most problems have been addressed and the remaining problems are chronic and will not change.

The management of communication at the government level has become more challenging because governments are being down-sized and decentralised.

Sustainable development is a complex concept dealing with the relationship between human development and ecological sustainability. The idea of sustainable development can be best communicated when broken into understandable components.

Constraints for communication. Within this context, communication faces constraints in capacity, policy relevance, and effectiveness. Among the first budgets to be cut in a recession are the communication budgets, losing capacity for communication and continuity of programmes. Capacity building for communication is essential, and especially so in emerging democracies.

Instruments such as education and communication are seen as the 'soft' side of policy development, and communication people are often not involved in the policy process.

People are beginning to distrust the messages they are receiving. Money is wasted on generalised messages that don't reach out to the required groups. Little research is done to see what message is reaching people at community level.

Being effective and strategic. A strategy is about changing people's practices and creating the right possibilities to do so. Therefore communication should be used in combination with other instruments, such as regulations and financial incentives. Putting the structures in place to support the change in behaviour makes it harder for people not to participate, and easier for those who are prepared to do so.

Communication is a management tool for policy. To successfully implement policy, communication has to be integrated into all phases of policy from agenda setting, through policy formulation, to implementation and control. Different tools in communication are used for different policy phases. To effectively communicate, it is important to know the stage of policy development. For example, in the policy identification stage, government can have a low profile, and communication is used to listen and gather information. One approach is to have staff that "surf the news", are able to spot interested journalists, and as they sit in on policy meetings can connect the journalists to leads and contacts on policy issues. At the policy-formulating stage, the government may become more active, and communication is a tool for the government to involve stakeholders. During the implementation stage, the government may use a communication strategy to reach key groups and mobilise their action and participation, through public service announcements on radio and television that can be picked up by the press and "constituency building" by providing assistance such as financial support for groups to work at community level. As society takes greater responsibility for the policy issue, the government can become less active, communication being used to maintain the support for the issue.

Some pointers to effective communication planning. The essence of a communication strategy is "do your homework" first. Other tips from the workshop include: analyse the issues; outline the role of communication; determine the target groups; identify and prioritise the specific needs of the target group; determine the communication targets; determine the strategy/message; determine the budget; build the capacity of the constituency; and evaluate.

Outputs and Follow-up

❏ Practical experience on communication which can be used in a publication on best practices for strategies for sustainability.

❏ Recommendations for building capacity for communication.

❏ Improved basis for communication between education and communication managers, strategy planners and international agencies.

❏ Exchange of experiences between communication managers from different regions.

Papers and Presentations

1. The Role of Communication in Achieving Canada's Environmental Policy (Ann Marie Smart, Environment Canada)

2. Essence of a Communication Strategy (Frits Hesselink, Chair, CEC)

3. Communication problems and solutions. Panellist introductions and responses: Dianne Brien, Great Barrier Reef Marine Park Authority; Dr Liana Talaue McManus, Marine Science Institute University in Bolinao, Philippines; Ms Ndey Njie, National Environment Agency, Gambia

4. Lessons learned from IUCN/UNESCO/UNEP regional workshops on national strategies for communication and education

    ❏ Lessons from Latin America (Denise Hamu de la Penha, Ministry of Environment, Natural Resources, and Amazon)

    ❏ Lessons from Asia (Kartikeya Sarabhai, Centre for Environment Education, India)

    ❏ Lessons from Europe (Peter Bos, Senior Officer, Strategy and Information, Ministry of Agriculture, Nature Management and Fisheries).

5.2 Key Issues in Good Practice for National-level Strategies

Organizer: IUCN Strategies for Sustainability Programme

Chair: Ndey Njie, Executive Director, the Gambia Environment Council

Rapporteur: Robert Prescott-Allen, PADATA, Canada

Summary

The purpose of the workshop was to review current practice in a wide range of strategy types at national level (NEAPs, NCS, Biodiversity Action Plans, Strategies to Combat Desertification) and through this review to identify the key issues and constraints to effective action. Over a decade of experience has been accumulated in developing and implementing strategies at national level. Many do not result in effective action on the ground, and instead end up as plans sitting on the shelf. Why is this and how can we try to ensure action? Strategy practitioners from Africa, Asia and Latin America and representatives of international agencies such as UNDP, UNSO and the World Bank concluded that in implementing strategies the link between national and local level needs to be strengthened considerably; time frames, goals and scope need to be more realistic; new initiatives need to be integrated with existing programmes; legal and institutional issues need to be addressed from the start; and strategies need to anticipate future changes (such as climate change) and not be stuck in the past.

Objectives

1. To review key issues in implementing strategies for sustainability at national level.

2. To highlight lessons learned for good practice in strategies.

Conclusions

Strengthen national-local links. Effective strategies are both top down and bottom up. Locally, governments are potentially a good vehicle for community participation. National governments need to include them in developing and implementing national strategies. Currently there is a gap between national and local strategies: national strategies fail to reach the ground, while local strategies fail to reach the top, even though many of the problems they try to address require intervention from the top.

Adopt realistic scope, timeframe and goals, and integrate with existing programmes. The design of the "model" strategy is over-ambitious and almost impossible for a national government to implement. Developing country strategies are usually funded externally, but only for periods that are far too short to accomplish the demanding tasks that have been set for them (e.g., 2–3 years). They need a few achievable goals and funding for an adequate period (e.g., 10 years). Funding should rely first on internal sources and only secondarily on external sources. Strategies should build on ongoing national programmes and plans.

Monitoring, assessment and communication are key. Engaging strategy teams in an assessment process can facilitate a vision of why a strategy process is needed, what to address in the strategy, and who should be involved in developing and implementing the strategy and what milestones should be used as indicators of progress. Communication skills are essential to the strategy process in order to develop and communicate clear messages targeted at behavioural change.

Address legal and institutional issues from the start. Legal issues range from the influence of the constitution on environmental conservation and sustainable development to providing a legal mandate to a coordinating body. Coordination and capacity building are the main institutional issues. Coordination includes the need for multilateral and bilateral agencies to harmonize their funding requirements, to make requirements and funding cycles more flexible, to shift from monitoring inputs to monitoring outputs, and to agree on a coordinating agency and allow it to coordinate them. It also includes using a national sustainable development strategy to provide a single response to the many international agreements rather than developing individual plans for each. Capacity building includes developing the skills to develop and implement strategies.

Focus more on anticipating and influencing the future. Most strategies lack vision and are stuck in the present. Therefore, they are unable to prepare countries for change. To anticipate and influence the future, they need to address emerging issues, develop scenarios, and enable people to explore a vision of the future and the kind of society and ecosystem they would like to have over the next 25 years.

Outputs and Follow-up

The key messages from the workshop will contribute to the Good Practices Guide on Developing and Implementing Strategies for Sustainability being developed by IUCN and strategy practitioners for use by governments, agencies and institutions who are developing and implementing multi-sector strategies aimed at sustainable development.

Papers and Presentations

1. Key issues, constraints and opportunities in the development and implementation of strategies (Mangetane Khalikane, Technical Advisor, Network for Environment and Sustainable Development in Africa; and Julius Chileshe, Facilitator for the IUCN Strategies Network, Africa)

2. Strategies Experience in Latin America (Alejandro Imbach, Facilitator for the IUCN Latin America Strategies Network)

3. Lesson Learned from Strategies in Bangladesh (Saleemul Huq, Executive Director, Bangladesh Centre for Advanced Studies)

4. Green Planning in Industrial Countries (Barry Dalal-Clayton, Director, Environmental Planning Group, International Institute for Environment and Development).

5. Constitutional Issues in Strategies (Alison Field-Juma, Associate Director, African Centre for Technology Studies)

6. Linking Global and Local Environmental initiatives (Mary Pattenden, Associate Director, International Council for Local Environmental Initiatives)

7. The Elusive Goal of Harmonization of Strategies (Karen Jorgensen, Assistant Director, Sustainable Energy and Environment Division (SEED), United Nations Development Programme)

8. The Importance of Linking National Frameworks to Local Action (Samuel Nyambi, Director, Office to Combat Desertification and Drought (UNSO/UNDP))

9. The World Bank and Strategies (Colin Rees, Director, Natural Resources, Lands and Water, Environment Division, The World Bank).

5.3 Strategies Experience at the Local Level

Organizer: IUCN Strategies for Sustainability Programme

Chair: Mohammad Rafiq, Director, Sarhad Provincial Conservation Strategy Pakistan.

Rapporteur: Arturo Lopez, Latin American Strategies Network member

Summary

IUCN, through the regional networks of strategy practitioners, has assessed experience in over 50 local strategies for sustainable development. A synthesis of their results, key issues and lessons learned was presented by the various speakers. Many experiences in local level strategies come from marginal socio-economic conditions in rural or suburban settings of developing countries. All these processes have addressed and achieved results in land-use planning, local participation and organization, capacity building, education and training. The most important concepts and components of local level strategies are: practical approaches to strategic planning, stakeholder analysis, participation, conflict resolution, intersectoral focus, and problem-focused analysis. A major question for local strategies is whether an island of sustainability can survive in an unsustainable world, and how local people can address externalities that have a profound affect on their lives. Recommendations included: political and administrative integration into the national level; economic equity; financial independence; continuity over time; tools such as better economic incentives, monitoring and evaluation of processes and results; and how to communicate at all levels.

Objectives

1. To analyse current practice in strategic planning initiatives at the local level.

2. To highlight key issues, trends and lessons learned in local level strategies.

3. To highlight key tools and methods, in particular where education and communication have been effectively used in local strategies.

Conclusions

Integrate local initiatives into national policies. Mechanisms to integrate local initiatives into national policies are lacking in most countries. Links may be provided through local-national committees, sharing of technical teams, or unions of local governments. Steering Committees should seek the endorsement of their resolutions by the national planning authorities. A national body should evaluate progress, and facilitate the same type of processes in other localities. If major decisions are taken at the national level that affect the lives of local people, then communities may reject them outright if they have not been involved. National governments should be facilitators for local action.

Consider externalities. Local strategies are heavily influenced by externalities – national and regional policies, trade, investment all impact heavily on local strategy teams. Strategies are not politically neutral – they empower local communities; they strive for land-use changes and adaptations in land-tenure schemes; and they advocate local ownership over local resources. Political commitment and support is important when substantial reforms are needed.

Continuity of the process. Continuity of the process depends on the commitment, degree of ownership and involvement of communities and NGOs in the strategy process. Financial self-sufficiency is also important; external funds may start the wheel turning but no strategy should become donor-dependant. Local resources must be mobilized. Continuity also requires economic and financial success. Sustainable production schemes need new incentives: internalization of environmental costs, developing markets for new products, and marketing in equity.

Focus on capacity building and training. To develop capacity, strategies must build on existing initiatives and structures and not duplicate other efforts. Emphasis should be given to capacity building where people are motivated to change their behaviour related to resource use practices. Decentralization empowers participation and capacity building. Local strategies provide many opportunities for formal and informal training for a wide range of key stakeholders in the process.

Common issues and goals must be identified. It is essential to define common goals and priorities with stakeholders and then agree on the roles to be played by each participant. Avoid segregating issues into resource sectors – agriculture, forestry, etc. Sound land-use planning principles and practices should be used to guide incentives and economic investment. Land-tenure and resource-tenure must be considered as well as cultural traditions and socio-economic capacities. Priority should be given to strengthening existing structures and initiatives, rather than starting new ones. Participation is the main tool to achieve a shared sense of responsibility; the entire process should be transparent from the beginning.

An engine to drive the process. An "engine" is needed to drive the process; strategic planning and communication expertise is necessary to lead the process, but teams should be as local as possible. Team members and experts may be used to replicate these processes in other locations. Planning processes must respect local knowledge. Results are important to retain the motivation and interest of stakeholders. Monitoring and evaluation is essential to keep the focus and evaluate the impacts of actions. Results and technical reports should not obsess the teams; it is the process of empowering people to take action that counts.

Cross-cutting issues

The importance of using gender analysis tools was recognized in the discussion as well as the adoption of an explicit gender and youth strategy in local sustainable development processes. Communication skills and capacities were acknowledged as crucial to local strategies in order to target and adapt messages to different audiences and cultures.

In most places, local strategies have no judicial framework within which to operate. The lack of an appropriate legal framework is often responsible for the weak link between national and local strategies; several speakers mentioned that there are many useful laws but frequently conflicting jurisdictions, overlapping mandates and responsibilities; there are many more laws than effective enforcement mechanisms.

Outputs and Follow-up

The key messages from the workshop will contribute to the Good Practices Guide on Developing and Implementing Strategies for Sustainability being developed by IUCN and strategy practitioners for use by governments, agencies and institutions who are developing and implementing multi-sector strategies aimed at sustainable development.

Papers and Presentations

1. Local Level Strategies in Latin America (Alejandro Imbach, Facilitator for the IUCN Latin America Strategies Network and Natalia Ortiz, Fundación Pro-Sierra Nevada de Santa Marta [FDSNSM])

2. Zimbabwe District Environmental Action Planning Programme [DEAP] (Sam Chimbuya, Technical Advisor, Zimbabwe DEAP and Z.A. Masiye, Zimbabwe DEAP Core Team, Government of Zimbabwe)

3. Tumkur District Integrated Resource Management Plan Karnataka State, India (Ashok Kumar, Development Alternatives, Bangalore)

4. Nepal Local Level Planning (Krishna Oli, Head, Local Environmental Planning, IUCN Nepal)

5. Costa Rica Arenal Conservation and Development Strategy (Claude J. Tremblay, Executive Director, Arenal Project Costa Rica and Daniel Malenfant)

6. Eco-quartier Citizens Programme, City of Montreal (Jean-Pierre Gauthier, Executive Assistant to the Mayor of Montreal)

7. Linking Local and National Initiatives (Samuel Nyambi, Director, Office to Combat Desertification and Drought [UNSO/UNDP]).

5.4 Reaching Target Audiences and Changing Behaviour: Effective Communication in Strategies

Organizer: Ashok Chatterjee for the Commission on Education and Communication

Chair: Frits Hesselink, Chair of CEC

Rapporteur: Ellen Leussink, SME Mileau Adviseurs Netherlands, CEC

Summary

This workshop demonstrated that communication is a social process about influencing human attitudes and practices. As human behaviour is multi-factorial and dependent on interactions between different social groups, communication has to be planned and managed to encompass a range of interactions. Communication is required to ensure that people responsible for providing services, facilities, or technologies, do so in a timely and effective way. Communication is an integral part of project design, implementation and evaluation. Projects can only be designed when the problem is defined clearly and the desired changes in practice are articulated and possible. Successful communication depends on doing your homework first. The workshop provided experience in what that homework entailed.

Objectives

1. To draw out lessons learned from managing communication programmes for a best practices guide on strategies for sustainability.

2. To demonstrate some practical steps to help strategy planners/communicators to better integrate communication as part of local strategies or projects.

3. To recommend action by IUCN and the Commission on Education and Communication.

Conclusions

Communication has a critical role in changing practice. Changing attitudes and practices is a strategic process that is facilitated by communication. Communication is a fundamental part of managing change and an integral part of a project or programme; it is not something added on. This concept of communication has little to do with the way our public mass media functions or a pre-occupation with videos, posters, and publications. Communication is first dependent on an ability to listen.

Communication can only be effective when the problem is clearly identified. It has to be clear what practice has to change to improve the situation and what those people or groups have to do in order to make the change. Communicators must identify the end behaviour that is desired, then check back on whether it is happening. Are the changes feasible for the target audience? Have the costs of the required actions been considered? Constraints and opportunities must be clearly identified prior to planning action. As decisions about resource use involve village, district, and regional sectors and departments, communication management is fundamental to enable these groups to work together. A key to success is feedback from the villages to the regional level and to the monitoring system.

Changing practice requires the right possibilities. Consider what has to be communicated to the groups who provide the infrastructure or services for the programme. If the services are not provided to support the behaviour change, effort will be wasted. In an immunization case study, multiple failures – in the health system, health management, supervisory levels and health delivery – all undermined the effort to immunize babies. In this case the communication strategy needed to address changes in the infrastructure and practice of all these subsystems to achieve the desired results.

Communication planning is complex. Too often communication is seen as one way – from wise sender to ignorant receiver – with little traffic in reverse. To listen is to know where to start and how to connect. A communication strategy may have to act on the beliefs of the target group, influence the peer group, and mobilize supporting adults and institutions. By creating a web of social support, behaviour change is more possible.

A cost-effective campaign through partnerships and alliances. Evidence from a survey of the population's knowledge and understanding of the environment provided the foundation of a campaign to improve recognition of the problems. An NGO, Moises Bertoni Fundacion (Paraguay), formed a strategic alliance with the Ministry of Education to make co-productions for the campaign at reduced costs. Official support was gained when the Ministry signed agreements with the media to do the campaign, a critical factor when funds are limited. Support was requested from well-known institutions to broaden the availability of the spots. Lessons learned from running this campaign were: use everyday language; use simple images and not abstract ones; enlist the right sponsorship to have access to prime time slots; project the messages towards national and regional themes; and encourage regional mass media to broadcast the material.

Capacity to communicate must be built. Key actors need to be trained in communication, particularly to overcome paternalistic attitudes by government extension officers. Skills to listen and manage community discussions are required, as is specialized training in the key resource management issues being addressed. For example, extension workers need to be trained so that they can help villagers analyze the consequences, causes and possible solutions to their priority problems and assist to prepare action plans.

Communicating environmental risks needs special skills. When people are at risk from environmental contamination, communication has to be open, trustworthy, realistic, correct and complete. People have their own perception of the risks and fears and these have to be taken into account. Organizational structures are required to ensure regular, timely and sequential communication; otherwise communication can be fragmented. Key opinion leaders and informants need to be well briefed continuously.

Communicating with different cultures. Communicating becomes more difficult across cultures with no common language or concept of the risks. Language differences present almost insurmountable communication barriers, even with translation or interpretation. Scientific concepts and terms for example do not readily translate into most aboriginal languages. Scientists tend to talk in technical terms for which there is no translation, emphasize the uncertainty of their findings and are cautious in their recommendations and conclusions, all of which make the audience suspicious.

Outputs and Follow-up

❑ A best practice guide for strategy planners which describes how communication should be incorporated in it.

❑ A Commission initiative to form alliances to draw attention to communication amongst the donor community, and to prepare guidelines for better integration of communication in projects and capacity development programmes.

Papers and Presentations

1. Lessons Learned About Communication Planning in Dealing with Contaminated Native Food with the Inuit, Canada and Other Cases (Mark Stiles)

2. Lessons From Paraguay Communication Programme (Edith Aisbey, Fundacion Moises Bertoni)

3. The Role of Communication in Integrated Coastal Management in the Tanga, Tanzania (Claudia Kawau, IUCN Tanga Coastal Resources Project)

4. Introduction to a Practical Session on Communication Planning (Ashok Chatterjee, in which participants worked through a planning exercise)

5. Building on International Communication Experience From Other Sectors: Such as Health and Water and Sanitation (Gerson da Cunha, India, and Ashok Chatterjee).

5.5 Monitoring and Assessing Progress towards Sustainability

Organizer: IUCN Strategies for Sustainability Programme

Chair: Terry Smutylo, Head, IDRC Evaluation Unit, Canada

Rapporteur: Fred Carden, Programme Officer, IDRC Evaluation Unit

Summary

Assessment, action and reflection are all part of a continuous cycle wherein assessment and reflection informs action. The IDRC-IUCN pilot work on user-oriented assessment methodologies illustrates this in the Zimbabwe District Environmental Action Planning process where assessment methodologies are key to informing the action planning and decision making process at district level. Monitoring and assessment are not end-of-pipe or one-off processes and we cannot assume that scientific "experts" know and understand the interactions between people and ecosystems. Participatory assessment processes in Colombia and India illustrate the importance of investing in understanding the problem in order to take effective action. Ultimately the challenge is to change human behaviour and attitudes. In engaging people in assessment we must understand the system (human-ecosystem interaction) in order to understand the parts. Sustainability assessments undertaken in British Columbia, Canada, and in the Wellbeing of Nations project illustrate how to link ecosystem assessment (state of environment reporting) with human development assessments (Human Development Index). Finally, it is critical that institutions and individuals develop the time and space for reflection in order to learn from assessments.

Objectives

1. To demonstrate a range of approaches, methods and tools for monitoring and assessment progress towards sustainability.

2. To highlight their use in the context of field practice, policy development and institutional assessment.

Conclusions

Monitoring and assessment are critical if we are to understand the problems and take effective action. In order to understand why people behave as they do with respect to the use and management of natural resources, we must invest in understanding the problem. This requires assessment methodologies that explore, using participatory methods, the nature of human-ecosystem interactions. Time for reflection and verification of assessment data and information must be built in order to challenge and test our own assumptions of the problem, and to remain open to new insights gained through participatory assessment processes.

Start with the system in order to understand the parts. We need to understand the big picture (the system) in order to understand the parts. Knowledge of the way the system works allows us to better address the impact that people have on ecosystems. Influencing and changing human behaviour is the fundamental challenge of sustainable development, thus assessment processes must strive to understand what motivates people to act the way they do, and target specific changes in human attitudes and behaviour.

Monitoring and assessment must be linked to decision making processes. The purpose of undertaking assessments should be to inform decision making, not solely to collect data. Once the problem is understood through assessments, and priority actions are determined, then assessment data and information should assist decision makers in taking action and provide indicators and milestones to track progress.

Assessment should be a cyclical processes. Assessment, action and reflection should form a continuous cycle that repeats over time. Assessment is not a one-off event, and it should be seen as an integral part of project and programme design and implementation.

Monitoring and assessment should be user-oriented and user-driven. *What* is to be assessed; *why* assess and *who* should be involved in assessment processes should be the opening questions for any assessment process. There is a danger that assessments becomes data driven and not user driven. This is especially true when carried out by scientists who consider themselves "experts". Comprehensive data on everything is not needed in order to take action. Community ownership is central to effective assessments. Users should develop their own indicators and then use scientific data as a way of verification or cross checking their perceptions. Since communities are not monolithic, stakeholder analysis tools are critical to determine the key users of assessment. Communication skills and capacity among assessment teams is critical to ensure that the assessment processes is effective.

Reflect and learn from experience. There is no point in carrying out assessments if institutions and individuals do not have the capacity to learn from them. Time, resources and space for reflection must be built in order to learn from experience and modify actions as we go along. It is critical that management reinforces the required modifications.

Link assessments through all levels: Practice informs policy and vice versa. Assessments carried out at local level should strive to inform national policy frameworks, and national assessments should be linked to local assessments as a means of verification and ground truthing. No matter how good assessment processes are, if they remain isolated at local level - or are not grounded in reality at national level, then their benefit will be minimized.

Cross-cutting issues

Gender and equity issues were implicit in the discussion of assessment, stakeholder analysis and user driven methods. Communication was viewed as critical to carrying out effective assessment processes, stakeholder analysis, communicating the results, linking with decision making, etc. The process of assessment is carried out in the context of political boundaries in order to inform the policy (and hence legal) processes.

Outputs and Follow-up

A greater understanding of assessment approaches, tools and methods based on pilot case studies will contribute to the section on monitoring and assessment in the Good Practices Guide on the Development and Implementation of Strategies for Sustainability. This guide is being developed by IUCN and strategy practitioners for use by governments, agencies and institutions who are designing and implementing multi-sector strategies aimed at sustainable development.

Papers and Presentations

1. Indicators of Sustainability (Peter Hardi, Senior Fellow, Director of Measurement and Indicators Program, International Institute for Sustainable Development)

2. IDRC/IUCN Work on Assessing Progress Toward Sustainability: Approaches, Methods and Tools: Overview (Adil Najam, International Assessment Team)

3. Pilot Country Experience: Zimbabwe (Sam Chimbuya, Technical Advisor, Zimbabwe DEAP and Masiye, Zimbabwe DEAP Core Team, Government of Zimbabwe)

4. Pilot Country Experience: Colombia (Natalia Ortiz, Fundación Pro-Sierra Nevada de Santa Marta, Colombia)

5. Pilot Country Experience: India (Ashok Kumar, Development Alternatives, India)

6. Assessing Sustainability at National Level: The Wellbeing of Nations (Robert Prescott-Allen, PADATA, Canada)

7. Sustainability Assessment: The Case of British Columbia, Canada (Tony Hodge, Member of the IUCN International Assessment Team and member of CORE, Government of British Columbia)

8. Institutional Learning: The Case of Capacity 21 (Howard Stewart, Advisor Capacity 21, UNDP).

5.6 Information Technology for Conservation: Tools for the 21st Century

Organizers: Kevin Grose, Alex de Sherbinin and Cécile Thiéry, IUCN

Chairs: Kevin Grose, Alex de Sherbinin

Rapporteur: Tim Lash

Summary

Case studies of current uses of information technology for conservation and sustainable resource use were presented and discussed. The cases showed effective use of available technology at scales of action from local to global. The major issues in further development of the technologies are social and institutional rather than technical.

Objectives

1. To raise awareness of emerging information and communication technologies and their potential to help achieve conservation and sustainable use objectives, particularly in environmental policy, strategies and planning.

2. Through case studies, to explore issues in the use of information technology for conservation and sustainable use of nature and natural resources, and to suggest effective approaches.

3. To demonstrate Internet, World Wide Web, Email, database, mapping, geographical information system and remote sensing technologies.

Conclusions

Current development of information technology is rapid and varied. The technologies are increasingly sophisticated, powerful, flexible, and able to interact with each other. Some can be adapted to individual and local needs, and to local use, design, and control. Some are explicitly designed to be simply and "democratically" used. The best, among a growing number of carefully-designed applications for conservation, include strong front-end definition of the local, national or global needs and problems being addressed, and put effort into communication of the results – to communities themselves, or to more aggregate-level decision makers.

Spatial information technologies, including remote sensing, Geographic Information Systems (GIS), Global Positioning Systems (GPS) and mapping, **can be strikingly effective for conservation when well-used**. Indigenous people have used GPS to demarcate traditional use areas and hence re-establish rights and interest in resource management in specific areas. Maps have the capacity to elucidate complex issues, and are a natural vehicle for communication (especially when posted publicly). GIS is a powerful tool in assessments, planning, negotiation and communication, easy to integrate with participatory planning.

The key issues in effective use are now social and institutional, rather than technical. For example:

❏ how to evolve collaboration and custodianship of data that respects partners' data interests, and engages their long term commitment to the shared enterprise;

❏ how to link data and data uses effectively from local through to global scales;

❏ how to mesh or interconnect various data bases among organizations, and how to avoid duplicating other global data base sets;

❏ how to pay for or charge for systems that add value to information or that make it available, while ensuring that the information is still affordable where it is needed;

❏ how to engage educators and students in gathering and using conservation information, without swamping data providers with school requests for information;

❏ what determines whether an information system, such as a list or news group on the Internet, is well-used or not;

❏ how to find out reliably what are the real and practical information needs of the users (or the information will not be used well);

❏ how to develop and maintain multiparty commitment to ongoing information systems.

People who are expected to use the information should be involved with the technology. They should also participate in the design, gathering, synthesis and use of the information in question. GIS and mapping will not work effectively until the people making the maps are the people who use them. There is a need to help users assess the quality of the information relative to its uses. People won't follow standards they have not helped to define and select. The challenge is to democratize GIS as a tool, by making it useful to people without extensive training.

Technology providers should thoroughly know the real questions, people, geographic realities that the information technologies are meant to serve. "The first thing a student should do is turn off the computer, and get into the field to get a feel of scale, learn what a hill is".

Information systems and data attributes should be selected and designed so the data are usable at different scales. Local vs global data is a false dichotomy, usually avoidable by paying attention to the need. Put local names, which embody local traditional knowledge, on maps which link upward. Use local people to ground truth information for higher level data sets. Share data readily between levels, rather than holding it back – those who have data should seek to share it with those who need it, and should use it to advise and develop data at the next higher level.

For applications **above the local level, new development should focus on regional or national conservation information instruments, or on particular global information specialities**, as there are now many general global database instruments. The *Biodiversity Conservation Information System* is an example of a global system that seeks to develop a specialized conservation focus in which data is owned and managed by those people or groups best able to do so – at the national, regional or global level – and made available globally over the Internet.

Cross-cutting issues

In one project area, where attention was paid to gender differences, the kinds of information identified by local women for mapping was significantly different from that identified by men. The differences may even require different map scales for gender-specific information – for example, women may give more spatially precise and descriptive local information related to the areas of cultivation.

Outputs and Follow-up

❏ The implementation of the **Biodiversity Conservation Information System**, including: coordination of BCIS development with other key biodiversity information initiatives (e.g. Clearing-House Mechanism of the Convention on Biological Diversity, CI, TNC, WRI, Species 2000, etc.); development of a full implementation proposal in collaboration with potential users and donors (e.g., World Bank); creation of a core secretariat to be housed at WCMC and recruitment of staff.

❏ IUCN/ELC and the Asia-Pacific Centre for Environmetal Law signed a memorandum of agreement on the exchange of environmental law data at the regional level.

❏ A workshop to explore how environmental assessment information can be made more widely available over the Internet.

❏ ICONS will be finalized following comments received and will be available free of charge from the IUCN WWW Site (http://iucn.org) and a pilot project in Central America is in preparation that will combine ICONS and Mapmaker.

❏ At IUCN Headquarters, a GIS and Conservation Group was formed to introduce staff to the principles and techniques of GIS and its application using some of the case studies demonstrated at the Congress.

Papers and Presentations

1. Background Paper: Union-Link: The IUCN Internet Presence (Kevin Grose, IUCN Information Management Group)

2. Union-Link: The IUCN Presence on the Internet (Kevin Grose)

3. Environmental Law Information System, and Environmental Treaties and Indicators Database (Nathan Sovik, Consortium for International Earth Science Information Network/ IUCN-Environmental Law Centre)

4. Database on Environmental Law (Lye Lin Heng and Charlotte Ong, Asia-Pacific Centre for Environmental Law)

5. International Environmental and Natural Resource Assessment Information System (INTERAISE) (Dan Tunstall, World Resources Institute/International Institute for Environment and Development/IUCN)

6. International Conservation Networking Software (ICONS) (Preston Hardison, Bill Harp and Julian Inglis, International Development Research Centre/IUCN)

7. Biodiversity Conservation Information System (BCIS) (Kevin Grose)

8. Capacity Building for Biodiversity Information Management (John Busby, World Conservation Monitoring Centre)

9. Advancing Conservation Through Biodiversity Information Management (Bruce Stein, The Nature Conservancy)

10. Biosphere Reserves Technical Training Project (Sean Gordon, Conservation International)

11. Report on 15-16 July,1996 International Workshop on Biodiversity Information (Jeff Waage, CAB International/IUBS/IUFRO/IUCN/UNEP)

12. GIS in Conservation (Alex de Sherbinin, IUCN)

13. Remote Sensing and Space Technology (Lawrence Gray, Canadian Space Agency)

14. Mapmaker in Colombia (Fernando Salazar, Fundación Pro-Sierra Nevada de Santa Marta)

15. Conservation Priority Setting Workshop Method and Results (Silvio Olivieri, Conservation International)

16. GPS and Indigenous People (Peter Poole, Local Earth Observation Project)

17. Mapmaker (Eric Dudley)

18. Information resources for strategies in Karnataka, India (George Varughese, Development Alternatives)

19. Africa Data Sampler (Dan Tunstall, World Resources Institute)

20. Rapid Ecological Assessment (Roger Sayre, The Nature Conservancy)

21. Biodiversity Map Library (Jeremy Harrison, World Conservation Monitoring Centre)

22. ELADA21: the electronic atlas of Agenda 21 (Djilali Benmouffok and Jean Lauriault, International Development Research Centre).

6.1 Collaborative Management for Conservation

Organizers: Grazia Borrini-Feyerabend and Meghan Golay, IUCN Social Policy Group

Chairs: Yves Renard, Fikret Berkes, Ashish Kothari, Joyce Wafula, Mark Freudenberger, Lea Scherl, Tariq Banuri

Rapporteurs: Mark Freudenberger, Doris Capistrano, Bijaya Kattel, Nicholas Winer, Ashish Kothari

Summary

Collaborative Management (CM) is becoming recognized as an effective approach to achieving conservation of natural resources. This workshop illustrated and discussed partnership agreements among governmental agencies, local users of natural resources and other stakeholders, and explored the sharing of functions, rights and responsibilities in natural resource management. It discussed how management partnerships can further the IUCN mission and be effectively incorporated into the work of the IUCN members, Commissions, staff and cooperating agencies. Particular attention was given to feasibility conditions, process steps, institutional arrangements and policies and legislation supportive to the development of effective CM agreements. The workshop included case presentations from 10 countries, an expert round-table, the first meeting of the Panel on Collaborative Management (henceforth formalized into a working group under CEESP) and working group sessions to design the IUCN work programme on CM over the next triennium and to finalize a CM Resolution.

Objectives

1. To illustrate to the membership of IUCN at the Congress the underlying principles, concepts and applications of collaborative management as an effective conservation approach.

2. To provide a forum to discuss how the collaborative management approach can further the IUCN mission and be effectively incorporated into the work of the IUCN members, Commissions, staff and cooperating agencies.

3. To review a programme of action on CM for IUCN over the next triennium, with particular attention to budget requirements and potential sources of funding.

4. To review and finalize a draft resolution on collaborative management for consideration and adoption by the World Conservation Congress.

5. To gather experiences and comments to finalize an IUCN Report on the "state of the art" on CM for conservation.

Conclusions

Two main IUCN "constituencies" were present at the workshop to discuss and highlight the potential of collaborative management (CM) processes. One rallies around CM as an effective and efficient way of managing natural resources. The other sees CM as a way of promoting equity in access to resources, for instance by legitimizing the participation of local and indigenous communities in the management of protected areas. These two broad aims can be mutually reinforcing, and many participants in the workshop commented positively on CM as a meeting point for both conservation and equity. Some professionals expressed concern that incorporating a variety of stakeholders in management does not constitute an alibi for governmental agencies to relinquish their responsibilities as caretakers of the environment for future generations. They stressed that multi-stakeholder agreements should not become an avenue for "lowest common denominator" decisions.

Collaborative management processes – in the variety of forms and circumstances in which they are found in different environments and societies – are powerful pathways towards both more effective and efficient management of natural resources and a more just and equitable share of the benefits deriving from it. As such, they are central to the mission of IUCN. They ought to be fully legitimized as a conservation approach and actively advocated.

The potential of CM for conservation is very large, spanning all sorts of ecosystems, natural resources and geo-political settings. Yet its potential is only lightly tapped. IUCN needs to take a leading role and devote sufficient resources to further the understanding of collaborative management processes in operational detail and to assist its members to apply them in both policy and practice. "Learning by doing" should be a fundamental component of such a process. A programme on Collaborative Management for Conservation should be pursued by IUCN in the 1997-99 triennium, given adequate resources, and centrally placed among both its global and decentralized activities.

Within the above overarching conclusions, the following specific issues were discussed in detail:

❏ **Equity:** special attention and support need to be provided to the disenfranchised sectors of society – outside and within communities (communities are anything but homogeneous!) – so that CM does not reproduce inequitable relationships of power or, worse, result in the poor losing rather than gaining access to resources. The disenfranchised should be involved in *framing the rules* of developing agreements and not only participate in events run by others.

❏ **History and culture**: CM approaches need to be aware of historical and socio-political settings and to build on traditional knowledge and institutions. Yet they should not remain uncritically wedded to them, as some communities have made choices detrimental to both resource conservation and their own long-term economic well-being.

❏ **Flexible incentives and mechanisms** (e.g., shareholding of the benefits of conservation initiatives, seasonal permits, mosaic zonation, enterprise development, etc.) need to be explored and used to fit the unique and changing conditions of each management site.

❏ **Long term approach**: slow, capillary, in-depth processes are needed for CM at the community level to build trust among different stakeholders and to craft the details of agreements which, to be successful, need to be carefully adapted to each context.

❏ **Effective facilitation**: at times local NGOs can provide this, but they should strive to remain impartial and not become stakeholders themselves. The role of intermediaries can be intrusive as well as facilitative.

- ❏ **Conflict management institutions**: topical support to manage specific conflicts is not sufficient. Support needs to function through time as new conflicts are bound to develop in real life partnerships. Also, conflicts need not be feared. They are often at the "creative roots" of CM agreements.

- ❏ **Conservation stakeholder**: somebody should always be present to defend the rights of future generations and natural resources!

- ❏ **Enterprise development**: very often (but not always) revenue generation is an essential element of a CM agreement. Diversification of means to achieve revenue should be promoted at a maximum to avoid heavy reliance on natural resources. Also, mechanisms by which income is directly related to conservation results should be identified and applied.

- ❏ **Diffusion of information and process transparency** are necessary conditions for the CM processes to function. Information sharing and democratizing access to relevant information can break the imbalance of power among stakeholders.

Cross-cutting issues

Gender issues were approached primarily through the context of defining stakeholders. It was recognized that equity is a key concern of CM and heterogeneity and inequality among the stakeholders need to be taken into account, along with their differential abilities to bear costs and derive benefits from CM arrangements. Disadvantaged groups need more intensive investments in capacity building to be able to participate and enter into genuine negotiation with other parties. This holds true for gender-related and intra-household inequalities.

Mechanisms for bridging and allowing communications to flow across user groups and stakeholders are essential to successful CM. Emphasis should be on enhancing opportunities for field-based exchange visits allowing peer groups to meet and share "learning by doing" experiences. It was also acknowledged that the media can play an important "watch dog" role and can be used extensively to encourage people, especially those with no interest in negotiating, to sit down at the table.

Legal frameworks can be an obstacle or a catalyst for CM and while supportive legal frameworks are not a precondition for collaborative management processes at the local level, the policy and legal aspects of CM need always to be taken in great consideration. Institutional arrangements define rights and responsibilities, structure the management of conflicts and define enforcement of rules. Customary communal tenure is not a panacea for conservation. External vested interests have exploited communal legal arrangements and gained access to protected resources by driving wedges and fomenting divisions within the community. Creative melding of private legal instruments and classical public instruments (e.g., stockholding entities for resource management) may offer flexible, market-based, legal approaches to CM.

Outputs and Follow-up

- ❏ Gathering of material and experiences in collaborative management to be incorporated into the "State of the Art" report in Collaborative Management to be published by IUCN in 1997.

- ❏ IUCN programme outline on CM for Conservation in the 1997–1999 triennium and identification of actors to carry out specific tasks.

❏ Resolution on Collaborative Management for Conservation discussed, revised and approved by the Congress.

❏ Formalized and expanded Working Group on Collaborative Management (sponsored by CEESP – the Commission on Environmental Economics and Social Policy, formerly CESP – and including members from other Commissions, such as CEL, WCPA, etc.).

❏ Assistance to the Union in following up on the CM resolution and in implementing the programme on CM outlined within it.

Papers and Presentations

1. Introduction (Yves Renard, Caribbean Natural Resources Institute)

2. Collaborative Management for Conservation: An Overview of Issues and Opportunities (Fikret Berkes, University of Manitoba, Canada)

3. On-going IUCN Initiatives (Grazia Borrini-Feyerabend, IUCN Social Policy Group)

4. Prospects for Joint Management of Protected Areas in India (Ashish Kothari, Indian Institute of Public Administration)

5. Collaborative Management of Wildlife and Forestry Resources in Mukogodo Forest, Laikipia District of Kenya (Joyce Wafula, Kenya Wildlife Service)

6. Community-Based Coastal Resource Management: The San Salvador Island Experience (Ed Tongson, Haribon Foundation, the Philippines)

7. The Sierra Nevada de Santa Marta Conservation Strategy: A Participatory Process (Guillermo Rodriguez, Fundación Pro Sierra Nevada de Santa Marta, Colombia)

8. Conservation with a Human Face, Video Presentation (Biksham Gujja, WWF International)

9. Co-Management Initiatives with Maori in the New Zealand Conservation Estate (Henrik Moller, University of Otago with Margaret Bragg, Jane Davis, and Todd Taeipa)

10. Conflict Management for Coastal Conservation: The Sufrieres, West Indies (Yves Renard, Caribbean Natural Resources Institute)

11. Collaborative Management and Community Rights in the Chobe Enclave of Northern Botswana (Nick Winer, Natural Resources Management Project, Botswana)

12. Collaborative Management in the Tuscany Islands: Law as an Opportunity (Andrea Simoncini, University of Florence, Italy)

13. Collaborative Management: The Ugandan Experiences (Arthur Mugisha, Uganda National Parks)

14. Protected Areas, People and Collaborative Management: Experiences from Nepal (Bijaya Kattel, Dept. of National Parks and Wildlife Conservation, Nepal).

During the session on Sunday, October 20, a round-table discussion between nine leading experts in collaborative management was held. The speakers were:

Doris Capistrano, Ford Foundation, Bangladesh

Mark Freudenberger, WWF-US

Augusta Henriques, Tiniguena, Guinea Bissau

Michael Horowitz, Institute for Development Anthropology, US

Marshall Murphree, Centre for Applied Social Sciences, Zimbabwe

Kishore Rao, CNPPA Vice Chair, Asia

Madhu Sarin, Society for the Promotion of Wasteland Development, India

Gustavo Suarez de Freitaz, CNPPA Vice Chair, Latin America

Marija Zupancic-Vicar, CNPPA Vice Chair, Europe

6.2 Water and Population Dynamics: Local Approaches to a Global Challenge

Organizers: Alex de Sherbinin, IUCN Social Policy Group
Catherine Marquette, Population Reference Bureau

Chair: Gayl Ness, IUCN

Rapporteur: Lisa Garbus

Summary

In an increasingly-populated world, and in a world seeking a higher quality of life through economic development, it is vital that water resources be managed efficiently and distributed equitably. Through nine country case studies and five expert presentations, this workshop examined the reciprocal links between water resources and population dynamics. A major focus was on participatory approaches to water resource management, and on improving institutional and policy arrangements governing the use and distribution of water for different sectors.

Objectives

1. To review and discuss the research findings of nine interdisciplinary country teams, each composed of one water resource expert and one population specialist.

2. To examine the "local-global" links between the case studies and global problems and trends, and to develop recommendations for improved policy and practice in the integrated area of water resources and population dynamics.

Conclusions

Avoidable and unavoidable pressure on water resources. In the future, there will be *avoidable* and *unavoidable* pressure on water resources. The *unavoidable* pressure comes from "population momentum" (the built-in growth due to young age structures) that in many countries will guarantee a doubling of population by 2025. Over the longer term, shortages can be *avoided* by taking swift action in the related areas of population policy, provision of reproductive health and family planning services, and improved educational and employment opportunities for women.

Population stabilization is vital, but will not eliminate water scarcity. Population stabilization reduces pressure on water resources and serves to "buy time" for the establishment of improved water management, appropriate policies and institutional arrangements, as well as the development and dissemination of appropriate technologies. However, population stabilization alone will not "solve" problems of water scarcity; these problems will persist until better institutions, policies and practices are in place.

Water resource issues benefit from a multidisciplinary approach. Water resource issues and population dynamics are not linked adequately to research, policy and practice. Due to disciplinary barriers and sectoral specialization, water resource specialists and population planners do not typically interact, let alone work together. Water resource issues can benefit from a multi-disciplinary team approach involving hydrologists, engineers, social scientists and ecologists who, together with local stakeholders, collaborate in all phases of problem identification and analysis, policy dialogue and formulation, programme design and management, enforcement, and monitoring and evaluation.

Local participation in water management can help redress inequities. Water is often "captured" by powerful economic interests, to the detriment of poor people. Access to water is a human rights issue, in as much as it is crucial for all aspects of human life. Collaborative management of water resources (i.e. power sharing between communities and state authorities) may be one mechanism for improving local resource management, especially in irrigation schemes. Furthermore, an objective and independent measure of the value of water resources leads to more efficient allocation, and, far from excluding the poor, can actually enhance their access.

Environmental conservation "versus" meeting human needs is a false dichotomy. Water-dependent natural ecosystems (e.g., wetlands, flood plains, and deltas) support highly productive fisheries, plant communities, woodlands, and agro-pastoral systems. Similarly, these wetlands directly and indirectly support large human populations. Thus for the millions of people worldwide who depend on wetland resources or benefit from wetland functions, providing water for the environment and for people is one and the same. This principle needs to be taken into account during the design and execution phases of large-scale dam and water-resource development projects. For dam projects, controlled flooding can sustain critical ecosystems while still accommodating other needs such as electricity generation, navigation, and irrigation.

Water-population links are location specific. The interplay between water resources and population dynamics is location-specific. Involving local communities in problem definition and throughout the process is crucial to understanding the local context and conditions, ensuring sustainable management of water resources, engendering a sense of ownership, and strengthening community capacity.

Proper institutions should be developed. In order to avoid conflict over water resources, water management arrangements need to be strengthened. Wherever possible, water resource management should take place within the context of existing institutions and power structures (e.g., national environmental agencies and ministries, water management boards, judicial systems, etc.), strengthening their technical capacity and institutional viability. Integrated river basin water management strategies should be developed for both single- and multi-country (i.e. transboundary) river basins, and harmonized with national sector-specific water development and population policies.

Public education is vital. Policy makers and the general public need to be educated about water resources and population dynamics, with the emphasis on adaptive mechanisms to manage human activities with respect to water resource constraints. Policy makers should be encouraged to participate in "South-South" and "South-North" exchanges and study tours in order to learn from successes (and failures) in water resource management. Communities and grass roots organizations require educational materials and training to improve their understanding of water resource issues. The materials and training should use a "systems approach" which includes an understanding of the downstream effects of certain kinds of water abstraction and use, as well as impacts on ecosystem functions.

Treaties are needed between riparian states. In single- and multi-country river basins there needs to be a recognition of upstream and downstream rights and responsibilities in river basin management, as well as the local interests involved. These should be reflected in treaties between riparian states or provinces. River basin authorities should be established for major river basins, and independent water commissions should be established (or strengthened) nationally. These authorities and commissions should be given the power to create and enforce policies while ensuring equity.

Outputs and Follow-up

1. A packet was produced for the workshop, including summaries of the country case studies, the agenda, and a list of contacts.

2. A workshop summary report, including selected policy recommendations and case study summaries, will be published by the Population Reference Bureau in early 1997.

3. A compilation of the case studies, expert presentations, and full policy recommendations will be published by the American Association for the Advancement of Science.

Papers and Presentations

1. Complexity in Water and Population Links (Malin Falkenmark, Sweden)

2. Water Supply and Mountain Systems (Jayanta Bandyopadhyay)

3. Participatory Approaches to River Basin Development (Thayer Scudder, USA)

4. Water and Population Dynamics in Tanzania (Basia Zaba)

5. Ten Principles of Water Management (Michael Acreman, UK)

6. India: Tumkur District, Karnataka (Ashok Kumar and K.C. Malhotra)

7. Pakistan: Rahuki Canal Area, Sindh Province (Aijaz Nizamani and Fauzia Rauf)

8. Morocco: Management of Irrigation in Northwestern Morocco (Abdelhadi Bennis and Houria Tazi Sadeq)

9. Mali: Population and the Problem of Water Supply (Hamady N'Djim and Bakary Doumbia)

10. Bangladesh: The Ganges Delta (Haroun Er Rashid and Babar Kabir)

11. Southern Africa: Emerging Competition for Water in the Zambezi River Basin (Roger Mpande and Michael Tawanda)

12. Jordan: The Azraq Oasis Conservation Project (Ghaith Fariz and Alia Hatough-Bouran)

13. Zambia: The Kafue Floods (Harry Chabwela and Wanga Mumba)

14. Guatemala: Water and Sanitation in the Peten (César Barrientos and Victor Fernandez).

6.3 Poverty, People and the Environment

Organizers: Angela Cropper, UNDP and Achim Steiner, IUCN-US

Chair: Angela Cropper; Achim Steiner

Rapporteurs: Eren Zink, IUCN-US

Summary

Consensus is growing among both conservationists and development workers that successful programmes and policies depend upon the recognition of the linkages between poor people and the environment. It is agreed that the traditional paradigm equating poverty with environmental degradation and conservation as a cost born disproportionately by the poor has proven counter-productive. In its stead has arisen the idea that conservation can be an asset in the creation of sustainable livelihoods for poor people. IUCN and UNDP invited speakers from diverse regions and backgrounds to examine experiences, policy options and technical supports that reinforce the new paradigm in this workshop on poverty, people and the environment. Specific topics discussed included technology, trade, agrobiodiversity, land reform and buffer zones.

Objectives

1. To review state of the art research and analysis of the linkages between poor people and their environment.

2. To move beyond the association of poor people with environmental degradation and examine the potential for linking conservation strategies to creation of incomes and livelihoods.

3. To discuss experiences, policy options and technical support in developing economic opportunities for poor people based on their role as primary users of natural resources.

4. To communicate issues, experiences and ideas in and among conservation and development professionals, policy makers and technical experts.

Conclusions

Sustainable livelihoods provide a reasonable income, are meaningful, do not cause environmental degradation and furnish a needed product or service. It is generally agreed that charity and government alone will not be able to satisfy this need.

Technology

While today's mass production technology may provide reasonable incomes to some, the benefits are more than offset by the costs. The technology often destroys the resource base and produces excess waste. Furthermore, it is far too expensive to accommodate large-scale poverty alleviation. Appropriate technology must be adapted to an area's particular social, economic and ecological environment. It must not be discriminatory to women or other groups. Hence, the goal of technology innovation is not the largest, fastest or "best," but rather the optimal.

The Indian corporation Development Alternatives, a leader in the creation of sustainable livelihoods through technical innovation and entrepreneurial support, shared several lessons learned with workshop participants. Production and sustainability can be improved by developing low-cost, low impact technologies adapted to small scale production. Microenterprises based on these technologies often employ more people and enjoy higher monetary returns per unit output than other means of production. As an added benefit, microenterprises keep, on average, 40% of their revenue within the local community, significantly more than the 5–8% that would be retained otherwise. Finally, providing training, franchising businesses and purchasing products that local economies do not consume helps ensure success and sustainability.

Markets

Sustainable livelihoods and biodiversity conservation are often mutually dependent upon national and international markets. It is not surprising then that we find both suffering where trade barriers have been erected.

Many countries are returning ownership of natural resources to the people who live with them. Local women and men have an incentive to practice conservation and sustainable use of these resources when markets are available. For example, in Zimbabwe CAMPFIRE areas earn more by conserving biodiversity (through craft production, use of wildlife and veld food trade) than they could under an exclusively agricultural or pastoral land-use system. Revenues accrued from the natural resource market can be instrumental in improving the lives of some of the world's poorest people.

Unfortunately, trade policy is sometimes at cross-purposes with poverty alleviation and conservation objectives. For example, CITES's closing of the ivory market has had an enormous cost for rural Africans.

As another example, the genetic diversity of the potato in Peru is threatened by the virtual disappearance of the market for all but a few fast-growing varieties. Because of economic necessity, the poor are forced to grow only these more productive potatoes. Some of the wealthier farmers, because of their success with fast-growing potatoes, are maintaining agrobiodiversity by producing the slower growing indigenous strains for consumption as a luxury good. However, if incomes are threatened, the demand for luxury potatoes will quickly disappear, and with it the genetic diversity of the species. No international market provides an incentive for the conservation of these potatoes because agricultural subsidies in the North make the unsubsidized Peruvian potatoes uncompetitive. Mechanisms that encourage farmers to maintain genetic diversity are needed everywhere.

Intellectual property rights

Intellectual Property Rights (IPRs) directly (and sometimes adversely) affect the creation of sustainable livelihoods. Are IPRs, as they are currently constituted, an obstruction to poverty alleviation and conservation objectives? The Convention on Biological Diversity calls for the "equitable sharing of benefits" from the use of genetic resources. Holders of traditional knowledge should benefit when industries use their knowledge about plant and animal species to develop products but this is not current practice. Pharmaceutical, agricultural, cosmetic, fabric industries, etc. continue to profit from the use of traditional knowledge. Under international IPR law these industries should be obligated to return a portion of their earnings to the holders of traditional knowledge. Such revenue could contribute to the creation of sustainable livelihoods and biodiversity conservation, much like the earnings from wildlife markets.

It is uncertain whether patents would be an acceptable incentive for holders of traditional knowledge. IPRs are, by nature, adapted to the needs of individuals and corporations. Traditional knowledge, on the other hand, is usually collective, making the distribution of benefits problematic. In addition, restricting production of alternative technologies with IPRs limits their distribution, and thus conflicts with the objective of creating as many sustainable livelihoods as possible.

Resource rights

Resource rights are a necessary foundation for the building of sustainable rural livelihoods. While state support is vital when attempting to secure resource rights for the poor, public policy alone cannot solve the problem. A local land tenure plan must be devised that accounts for local realities and protects the natural resource base while raising productivity and revenue. The presence of technical partners and accountable, transparent institutions is also important for success. Involving stakeholders in plan development defuses the potential for destructive conflict later, provides insights on the establishment of appropriate socio-economic infrastructures, helps identify the most important problems and suggests solutions, and involves young people, which increases sustainability.

Where these processes have been carried out, the results have been favorable. A forestry management project sponsored by the UNDP is an excellent example, where women with rights to forested land are sustainably harvesting wood which they then use as an economic basis for improving their lives.

Buffer zone management

A combination of local, national and international organizations can reconcile conservation with poverty alleviation and show that greater success is possible when there is cooperation between various levels of organization rather than domination by one. The strategies found most successful include:

❏ involving and strengthening local organizations

❏ increasing organizations' participation in decision making

❏ sustainably increasing local production

❏ using appropriate local technologies for sustainable use of natural resources

- establishing strategic alliances between involved sectors

- working by consensus and compromise

- recognizing and addressing the contradiction between short-term poverty alleviation goals and long-term conservation goals.

Cross-cutting issues

Experiences in the field emphasized the need for programmes and policies that give particular attention to the issue of gender. For example, Development Alternatives demands that their technologies do not create or reinforce gender discrimination. Trade, land or conservation policies and programmes that do not incorporate the concerns of both genders will suffer ill effects, much like those under the traditional conservation and development paradigm. Experience with peasant communities in the Andes was a poignant example of the necessity to explore gender roles in a community. In the Peruvian Andes, households have three economies. One is primarily controlled by women, one by men and one jointly. A policy that does not address all three will likely fail.

Actors at the policy-making level need to communicate with those at the community and programme level. Lack of communication partially explains policies at cross purposes with conservation and development objectives. Furthermore, policy-makers in national capitals cannot expect to be successful without communication with affected localities.

Some laws can be detrimental to the cause of poverty alleviation and environmental conservation. Environmental law restricting trade in natural resources can hasten the demise of that which it intends to save. The creation of sustainable livelihoods depends upon the ability of lawmakers to adopt the new development and conservation paradigm addressed during this workshop. It also requires lawmakers to take a more holistic view of environmental law. For example, intellectual property rights law can no longer be thought of simply in terms of its effects on trade; it has much wider implications for conservation and poverty alleviation. Law also plays a central role in codifying resource rights and collaborative management regimes.

Outputs and Follow-up

UNDP and IUCN are collaborating to publish the proceedings of the "Poverty, People and the Environment" Workshop. UNDP is preparing further case studies and policy guidelines of Rio+5 events in 1997.

Papers and Presentations

1. Sustainable Technology and Poverty Alleviation (Ashok Khosla, Development Alternatives Inc., India)

2. Biodiversity as an Asset and Constraint to Poverty Alleviation (Manuel Glave, Grupo de Analisis para el Desarollo, Peru)

3. Alleviation of Poverty and Environmentally Sustainable Development: The Role of International Markets, Trade and Conventions (Langford Chitsike, Africa Resources Trust, Zimbabwe)

4. La Gestion des Terroirs comme Stratégie Contribuant à l'Accès aux Ressources Naturelles par les Populations Déshéritées (Albertine Darga, Programme National de Gestion des Terroirs, Burkina Faso)

5. Corredor Biologico Talamanca Caribe (Rosa Bustillo, Talamanca Corridor Protected Area, Costa Rica).

6.4 Ethics in Conservation Biology

Organizers: Catherine Potvin and Gilles Seutin, McGill University

Chairs: Catherine Potvin and Gilles Seutin

Rapporteur: Rogelio Cansari

Summary

Conserving biological diversity presents important ethical challenges, so conservation biology would benefit from having a code of ethics. The notion of informed consent was proposed as a basis to inform and involve local populations in conservation action. Respect of national and local legislation as well as customary practices and local value systems were seen as critically important. The need to share results with local communities was repeatedly stressed.

Objectives

1. To assess the need for a professional ethic of conservation biology.

2. To identify elements of a code of ethics for practicing conservation biologists.

3. To identify good and bad attitudes of foreign scientists involved in international collaborations.

4. To examine the needs, expectations and priorities of conservationists, natural resource managers and scientists from developing countries.

Conclusions

A philosophical basis. Conservation biology is a relatively young science that does not yet have a clear philosophical basis. To solve the tension between environmentalism and anthropocentrism, it was proposed to move toward the recognition of a dialectical relationship between culture and nature. At a more practical level, an analogy was made between conservation biology and medicine that allows elements of a code of ethics for conservation biologists to be identified. Diagnostic of environmental degradation and decisions on remedial actions are the basis of the analogy. An important suggestion was that steps toward remedial actions require "prior informed consent." The idea of "informed consent" provides a philosophical basis and a conceptual framework for the current tendency of favouring grass-root actions in conservation. However, several questions still need to be answered: Whose consent is required? How should it be requested? Respect of national and local legislation as well as customary practices were elements of the answer. The analogy with medicine also raised the difficult issue of confidentiality.

Specific expectations and attitudes: Respect. One cannot cure the environment without curing human populations. Just as "appropriate" attitudes are key to successful development initiatives, they are essential to progress in conservation. Fostering respect for all parties involved in a collaboration was deemed essential. Respect involves sharing information with local populations, avoiding false promises, acknowledging contributions to research through authorship, etc. In this context, the question of the relative status of national scientists and international experts was discussed.

Community involvement. The need for a strong involvement of local populations was mentioned by all speakers. It was actually suggested by some that conservation actions should never be undertaken without the local populations being in charge. While the discussion was focused on international collaborations, national biologists were also often insensitive to the needs of local populations. Thus, ethical guidelines would be equally useful in that context.

Modes of intervention. While 50–90% of the total biological diversity is found in the tropics, only 7% of the world's ecologists come from that zone. Thus, there is a great need for international scientific exchanges. Short visits of experts is currently the predominant mode of international collaboration in environmental issues. While such missions might allow specific biological problems to be addressed, they typically do not permit a full comprehension of the complex interactions between nature and local populations. Thus, proposed solutions will often be inadequate or inefficient. Proposed alternatives: to pair off international experts with national scientists aware of the larger issues; or to favour foreign scientists with long-term commitment to specific areas and problems.

Cross-cutting issues

Special attention was given to "gender issues". Interestingly, two points of view were advanced. Some suggested that any international collaboration in conservation biology should be beneficial to, and should involve, women. Others held that local attitudes toward women should be respected and that any foreign initiatives attempting to modify the status of women in their society was a form of colonialism and, thus, unethical. The persons presenting these opposing points of view were both women.

Outputs and Follow-up

❏ Publication of a scientific paper summarizing the ideas emerging from the workshop

❏ Publication of the proceedings as an edited book.

Papers and Presentations

1. Welcome and Introduction (Gilles Seutin, McGill University)

2. Anthropocentrism and Non-anthropocentrism: Implications for the International Agenda (Bryan Norton, Georgia Institute of Technology)

3. Quelle éthique pour les biologistes de la conservation? (Marie-Hélène Parizeau, McGill University)

4. Effectiveness and Empowerment in Environmental Aid (Georgina Wigley; CIDA)

5. Aménagement et gestion des aires protégées tropicales et opportunité d'un code d'éthique ayant trait à la recherche collaborative en Afrique: cas du Zaïre (Léonard Mubalama, Institut Zairois pour la Conservation de la Nature)

6. Perspective d'une scientifique concernant la pratique et la gestion des problèmes de conservation biologique: cas du Madagascar (Lala Henriette Rakotovao, Conseil National de Recherche sur l'Environnement)

7. Achieving Conservation through Pride (Victor Regis, RARE Centre for Tropical Conservation, St Lucia)

8. A Synthesis (Catherine Potvin, McGill University).

7.1 Incentives and Disincentives for Conservation

Organizers: IUCN's Biodiversity Programme, Center for International Environmental Law (CIEL)

Chair: Hon. Gerald Sendaula, Minister of Natural Resources, Uganda

Rapporteurs: Jill Blockhus, Frank Vorhies

Summary

This workshop opened a stream of workshops at the World Conservation Congress called "Using Economics as a Tool for Conservation". The workshop consisted of several presentations and case studies on the use of incentive measures for the conservation and sustainable use of biological resources. Discussion focused in particular on the use of incentive measures in the context of the Convention on Biological Diversity. The workshop discussed the widespread problem of perverse incentives, which discourage conservation and sustainable use.

Objectives

1. To provide an opportunity for the IUCN Membership to explore the use of incentive measures for biodiversity as called for in Article 11 of the Convention on Biological Diversity.

2. To provide insights for future work in this area by the IUCN Secretariat, the Commissions and the Membership.

Conclusions

The workshop began with a report back on the incentives workshop at the 4th session of the Global Biodiversity Forum (GBF) which took place in August/September 1996 in Montreal. The GBF workshop recommended to: 1) Recognize that economic valuation is not a prerequisite for effective implementation of incentive measures; 2) identify and remove perverse incentives; 3) establish legal and institutional frameworks that support effective implementation of incentive measures; 4) secure property rights (for local and indigenous communities) over biological resources; 5) involve local and indigenous communities and incorporate their knowledge and needs; 6) incorporate equity considerations in the implementation of incentive measures; and 7) ensure long-term financial and institutional sustainability.

Other presentations focused on perverse subsidies, and looked at cost-effective ways of conservation through subsidy reform; focused on making ecotourism a positive incentive for conservation; reviewed a regional approach to conserve wildlife habitats, particularly for songbird species; identified a large market for non-consumptive uses of biological resources, and tapping this market by taxing certain goods tied to birdwatching in order to raise money for conserving bird habitats; and proposed an institutional framework for addressing incentive measures by looking at the legal, social and compliance or enforcement end of the spectrum. Following every presentation was a lively discussion of the issues.

The key message from the presentations and the discussions indicated that further work on incentive measures would provide a great opportunity for conserving biodiversity. This includes work at the community level – affecting change on the ground – which involves changing people's behaviour. Some of the major areas of concentration include reforming property rights, allowing for access to resources, and creating markets for certain products (e.g., non-timber forest products) which might not have existed. More specific conclusions:

Incentives for biodiversity. Incentives can play an important role for conservation and sustainable use of biological resources, especially in the context of the implementation of Article 11 of the Convention on Biological Diversity. The IUCN Secretariat, its Commissions and its Members have a real opportunity to design, apply and monitor the use of incentive measures.

Removal of perverse incentives. A major threat to sustainable development is the widespread existence of perverse incentives that encourage actors to carry out activities which are counter to the objectives of sustainable development. In particular, perverse subsidies are of concern because they encourage bad practices and redirect scarce public funds to work in the wrong direction. Thus a special effort is needed to understand and address the impacts of perverse subsidies. This is equally applicable for biodiversity considerations as it is for other dimensions of the sustainable development agenda. In its policy and project work, IUCN should pay special attention to dealing with perverse incentives.

Managing tourism as an incentive for biodiversity. The management, regulation and taxation of tourist activities can encourage the conservation and sustainable use of biological resources. So-called "ecotourism" and the design of measures to ensure that ecotourism revenues are directed in support of biodiversity offer particular opportunities for engaging the private sector and local communities in biodiversity conservation. Careful attention needs to be paid to the structure of tourism policies and practices to ensure that tourism acts in support of biodiversity instead of to its detriment. With IUCN's emerging interest in the private sector, the tourism industry is one sector that deserves particular attention.

The institutional dimensions of incentive measures. Incentive measures as envisioned by the Convention on Biological Diversity are much more than economic instruments. Yes, the measures must make economic sense, but they must also be socially and politically acceptable. In addition, the strength of social and legal institutions to ensure compliance with these measures cannot be ignored. In this context, the workshop noted that incentive measures cannot be grouped into economic incentives, social incentives, legal incentives, and so on, but rather that the design and implementation of incentive measures requires serious consideration of the social, political, legal and economic institutional framework in which they must operate. This recognition made clear the need for IUCN to strive for an integrated approach to conservation management, especially in bringing legal, economic and social expertise together with traditional scientific expertise in the design of policies, programmes and projects for biodiversity.

Cross-cutting issues

Gender did not enter into the discussions. Nevertheless, as many harvesters of biological resources in local and indigenous communities are women, appropriate incentive measure programmes for on-the-ground conservation cannot be designed without incorporating gender considerations.

Clearly, many things are happening out there on incentives. More progress could be made if we could share experiences on specific cases. After finding good examples (particularly on the application of incentive measures) we should do our best to get the message across to our members and partners.

Outputs and Follow-up

❑ Workshop report and papers will be placed on the IUCN Economics of Biological Diversity web site by mid-1997.

❑ Incentive measures for conserving biodiversity will be a major focus for IUCN's Biodiversity Programme in the coming triennium.

❑ Incentive measures is also emerging as a cross-cutting theme in much of the work of IUCN, its Members and its Commissions.

Papers and Presentations

1. Report on the Incentives Workshop at the 4th Session of the Global Biodiversity Forum (Jean-Didier Oth, Institut des Sciences de l'Environnement, Montreal)

2. Current Research on Perverse Subsidies (André de Moor, Institute for Research on Public Expenditure)

3. Economic and Sustainable Development Dimensions of Ecotourism (Hector Ceballos, CNPPA)

4. The Use of Economic Incentives to Protect Wildlife Habitat (Linda Duncan, NAFTA Commission on Environmental Cooperation)

5. The Economics of Bird Watching (Kathleen Rogers, Audubon Society, USA)

6. An Institutional Perspective on Incentive Measures (Stephanie Presbar James, presented by Alex James, University of Cambridge, UK)

7. Mainstreaming Economics as a Tool for Conservation (Frank Vorhies, IUCN).

7.2 Debt-for-Conservation Swaps

Organizers: World Wildlife Fund (WWF); Eurodad

Chair: Minister Jean Prosper Koyo, Congo

Rapporteurs: Jill Blockhus, Frank Vorhies, IUCN

Summary

A few years ago there was a good deal of interest in securing funding for conservation through debt-for-nature or debt-for-conservation swaps. Though the initial enthusiasm has diminished somewhat, debt remains a serious problem in many developing countries and conservation remains an obvious target for swaps. IUCN, with its unique members of states, government organizations, and non-governmental organizations, has a real opportunity to broker debt swaps for its members in support of conservation on the ground. Debt swaps are an exciting prospect for new and additional financial resource for financing conservation. They are and will continue to be of great interest to the IUCN constituency.

Objectives

1. To provide an opportunity for the IUCN membership to explore the use of debt swaps for conservation in the work of the broader IUCN conservation community.

2. To discuss the use of debt swaps for conservation in the context of broader development objectives.

Conclusions

A developing country perspective. Many developing countries, especially in this period of economic liberalization, see their debt situation as a major hindrance to economic development. Furthermore, the debt is having serious negative impacts on the environment, including over-exploitation of natural resources, deforestation, and soil erosion. Thus the debt acts as a perverse incentive working against sustainable development. By linking a debt swap to conservation, we may be able to turn a perverse incentive into an enabling incentive. Hence from a developing country perspective, the proposed IUCN resolutions on debt and the involvement of IUCN in debt swaps is most welcome.

Learning to swap debt for conservation. The language of debt swaps or debt conversion is filled with its own jargon, including concepts like debt structure, debt repurchase, secondary market, and redemption price, which are unfamiliar to many conservationists. Nevertheless, once the language is learned, the technique of converting debt for conservation is not complicated. Furthermore, the ability to carry out swaps efficiently and profitably comes from practice and from learning from other experiences. Thus the challenge for IUCN and is membership is not to learn how to do it, but rather to do it. The sooner we begin to engage in this process, the more professional we will become. This in turn will increase the demand to use our services and thus convert debt for conservation in support of sustainable development.

Learning from case studies. The case studies from Mexico, Peru, and Madagascar presented in the workshop showed how competency in debt swap transactions can be strengthened through case study analysis. They also showed the multi-institutional nature of debt swaps and the clear opportunities for both governments and non-government organizations to work together to ensure that debt conversions are used effectively for conservation,.

Highly-indebted poor countries (HIPC). Though debt swaps are a possible instrument for most developing countries, they have a special potential in highly-indebted poor countries (HIPC). In many cases, these countries are also especially well-endowed with biological diversity. Thus they have a tangible asset – biodiversity conservation – to swap for their debt obligations. As IUCN and many of its members are working in these countries, special consideration should be given to debt-for-conservation swaps in these countries.

Cross-cutting issues

In negotiations for debt settlement, a series of contractual deals will require proper legal documentation. Here is a real opportunity for environmental lawyers, such as those working in the IUCN Environmental Law Centre.

Outputs and Follow-up

❏ Workshop report and papers to be placed on the IUCN Economics of Biological Diversity web site by mid-1997.

❏ Debt swaps for conservation is clearly a financial tool for much of the work of IUCN and requires the Secretariat to maintain technical expertise in this area.

Papers and Presentations

1. Past Debt Management Policies and Strategies (Daouda Bayili, Minister of Budget, Burkino Faso)

2. Introduction to Debt Conversion Theory and Techniques (Alain Lambert, IUCN)

3. Case Studies (Marianne Guerin-McManus, Conservation International, USA)

4. Case Studies (Randy Curtis, The Nature Conservancy, USA)

5. The Multilateral Debt: Up-To-Date Information (Ted van Hees, Eurodad).

7.3 Consumption Patterns

Organizers: Svenska Naturskydds Foreningen (SNF)

Chair: Goran Eklof

Rapporteurs: Jill Blockhus, Frank Vorhies

Summary

Global economic integration will increase the risk of sudden and rapid economic destabilization, but global economic integration is inevitable. The conservation community often focuses on the supply side of conservation, for example, by addressing the management of protected areas or the preservation of endangered species. But in a global economy there is both supply and demand, production and consumption. And in an increasingly global economy, consumption in the North influences production in the South. This workshop investigated the impact of northern demand or consumption patterns on the conservation of nature and natural resources, concluding that equity is a central principle towards attaining sustainability.

Objectives

1. To provide an opportunity for the IUCN membership to explore the demand side of conservation – the impact of consumption patterns on the conservation of nature and natural resources.

2. To define ways for IUCN to address consumption issues.

Conclusions

A challenging question is how can fertility be "decoupled" from the cultural complex in developing countries, where an inverse relationship exists between environmental awareness and environmental action.

Some points on sustainability. The following framework was presented for IUCN to consider in order to begin to address consumption and production issues in a comprehensive manner:

1. Environment and development crises are parts of the same phenomenon arising from global and national social, economic and cultural structures.

2. Resource depletion and contamination are too serious to allow "business as usual".

3. Equity is the central principle to "operationalize" and attain sustainability.

4. The present crisis is generated by the unsustainable economic model in the North, inappropriate development patterns in the South, and an inequitable global economic system that links the northern and southern models.

5. Many environmentally and socially appropriate technologies exist in the South.

6. It is not the poor who have destroyed the environment, but rather the affluent.

7. Given the gross inequities that exist, advocating universal solutions (such as "let us all together reduce consumption to save the Earth") can be misleading and dangerous.

8. Environmental sustainability, social equity and a culture that allows people to fulfil human needs are all integrally linked.

9. On the struggle towards environmental sustainability and social equity, action is needed at both local and global levels.

The World is a third world country. The population of the world and the global challenges for sustainable development all lie in the South. It is a mistake to think that the North must teach and the South must learn, when the real lessons to be learned come from the South. Neither the cultural system in the North nor that in the South is sustainable, and both must adapt and learn from the other. A feature of this is to understand the interrelationship between population and consumption, and how they influence conservation. Hence population and consumption issues are important to the work of IUCN.

Campaigning for sustainable consumption practices. There have been campaigns both in the North and the South promoting sustainable consumption practices. These have included promotion of the use of eco-labelling schemes and organic farming. Much analysis is still needed of these campaigns and of the tools they have advocated for improving consumption patterns. IUCN could support such efforts to improve our understanding of the role of consumption in conservation as well as the options available to promote sustainable consumption patterns.

Cross-cutting issues

Increasing the educational levels of women directly affects population rates. Some participants characterized the "invasive thinking" or "authoritarian" way of thinking as masculine (and thereby associated with the North).

The distinction between awareness, rhetoric and action needs to be considered when developing campaigns to influence consumption patterns and policies.

Outputs and Follow-up

❏ Workshop report and papers to be placed on the IUCN Economics of Biological Diversity web site by mid-1997.

❏ Consumption patterns is clearly of interest to part of the IUCN constituency and thus the Secretariat needs to consider carefully how to incorporate consumption issues into its programme of work.

Papers and Presentations

1. Sustainable Consumption and Production: Agenda 21 Chapter 4 with Particular Focus on Biodiversity (Meena Raman, Consumers Association of Penang, Malaysia)

2. Consumption and Population (Tariq Banuri, Sustainable Development Policy Institute, Pakistan)

3. The Shop and Act Green Campaign (Eva Eiderstrom, Swedish Society for Nature Conservation)

4. Consumer Campaigning and particularly Giant Shrimp (Meena Raman, Consumers Association of Penang, Malaysia)

5. Bananas and Coffee (Goran Eklof, Swedish Society for Nature)

6. Conservation with Assistance (Bernward Geier, IFOAM)

7. Conclusion and General Summary (Gunnel Hendman, Swedish Society for Nature).

7.4 Assessing Protected Area Benefits

Organizers: IUCN World Commission on Protected Areas (formerly the Commission on National Parks and Protected Areas)

Chair: Lee Thomas, Australia

Rapporteurs: Jill Blockhus, Frank Vorhies

Summary

The World Commission on Protected Areas (WCPA) – formerly known as the Commission on National Parks and Protected Areas (CNPPA) – has established a task force to develop a methodology for assessing the economic benefits of protected areas. This task force developed draft guidelines which were the focus of this workshop and on which comments were invited. In addition, the workshop looked at recent economic benefit studies and the work of WCMC in estimating and analysing global investments in protected areas. Investment in parks and protected areas is influenced by national income, biological richness, population density, and mean protected area size. Economic benefits of protected areas have two distinct aspects: first, the economic rationale for protected areas; second, providing economic advice for managing protected areas. A key challenge identified by the workshop was how to link the economic benefits of protected areas to their financial sustainability.

Objectives

1. To provide an opportunity for the IUCN membership to explore the use of economic tools to assess the benefits of protected areas.

2. To review the draft guidelines for assessing the economic benefits of protected areas developed by the World Commission on Protected Areas (WCPA).

Conclusions

Environmental Valuation Reference Inventory (EVRI). A considerable amount of work has been done on the economic value of ecosystems, natural resources, and parks which may be of use to protected areas. Environment Canada is now leading a major effort to collect these studies, assess them and store them in a well-structured, accessible Web-based inventory. Once this inventory is operational and contains a significant number of studies, it could be of use to protected area authorities and others interested in assessing the benefits of protected areas. IUCN and the WCPA may want to explore linkages between this project and the emerging Biodiversity Conservation Information System (BCIS).

A global perspective on investments in protected areas. The World Conservation Monitoring Centre (WCMC) has commissioned a major study on the financial and staff investments in protected areas. An analysis of the data indicates that budgets for protected areas is positively related to the national per capita income and, interestingly, is negatively related to the value of biodiversity in the country. Also, expenditures per hectare decline for larger areas, indicating the expense of managing systems of fragmented protected areas.

In addition, an attempt was made to determine whether actual budgets were adequate and estimates were made about the approximate size of the short fall. On a square kilometre basis, actual spending is at US$161, but ideal spending is at $436 and thus the shortfall is $275. This indicates a clear need for new and additional finances for the world's protected areas. IUCN should consider focusing on the financial needs of protected areas.

The WCPA draft assessment guidelines. The WCPA draft assessment guidelines are intended to help protected area authorities assess the economic impact of protect areas, including tourism, water production, fish breeding, etc. In so doing, the guidelines begin a process whereby the value of protected areas can be incorporated into national planning and national accounts. The workshop found that protected areas were in need of two different, but closely related approaches. The first is to assess the value of protected areas to the economy and thus to the nation. The second is to generate adequate revenues to ensure that protected areas will be properly maintained and managed. The former in a sense is used to justify the existence of parks, while the latter focuses on the sustainability of existing systems of protected areas. Clearly both areas are important and deserve further attention by IUCN, the WCPA, members and partners.

Outputs and Follow-up

❑ Workshop report and papers to be placed on the IUCN Economics of Biological Diversity web site by mid-1997.

❑ Promotion of a WWW site (called the Economic Valuation Reference Inventory, or EVRI) which aims to provide information on economic valuation studies around the world.

❑ WCPA to further explore the economics of managing protected areas, including development of a sustainable finance initiative for protected areas.

Papers and Presentations

1. The Environmental Valuation Reference Inventory (EVRI) (Fern Filion and Jim Frehs, Environment Canada)

2. Investments in Protected Areas (Alex James, University of Cambridge, UK)

3. The CNPPA Draft Assessment Guidelines (Francis Grey)

4. Comments on the Guidelines (G. Creamers)

5. Applying the Guidelines in Canada (Tatania Stroud).

7.5 Green National Accounts

Organizers: WWF and IUCN-US

Chair: Joy Hecht, IUCN-US

Rapporteurs: Jill Blockhus, Frank Vorhies, IUCN

Summary

Linking economics and the environment remains one of the key challenges to conservation. This workshop focused on key issues and practical experiences in addressing one of the strategic instruments in national development planning: the System of National Accounts (SNA). It showed how greening the SNA is an important objective in changing the parameters for sustainable development. The workshop focused on practical aspects of reforming the SNA drawing upon national experiences and case studies from institutions and initiatives in the field. It included two presentations on broad international considerations related to integrated economic and environmental accounting, and three on specific countries or regions.

Objectives

1. To provide participants with an overview of the issues, as well as insights from a practitioner's perspective as to how such SNA reforms have been initiated in a number of countries.

2. To consider the future work programme of IUCN in green accounting.

Conclusions

Growing support for green accounting. Modification of the SNA to integrate environmental considerations is necessary because the current system does not accurately account for use of environmental capital to generate income. Efforts by the international community began building momentum in the 1980s, with UNEP's work on the usefulness of national income accounting as a policy tool. In 1993 the UN published a handbook on integrated environmental accounting, and by now some thirty countries have experimented with it in some form. Support for this work has grown in recent years. The European Parliament has called for its implementation, which is now targeted to occur after monetary union. A conference held in Washington in 1995 led to the creation of an international working group on the topic, including the World Bank, IMF, various UN agencies, IUCN, the World Wildlife Fund, the National Wildlife Federation, and other groups. The group agreed on a joint work plan which includes additional country case studies, training of trainers, policy applications of environmental accounting, and further improvement in methodologies.

A view from the World Bank. The World Bank seeks to incorporate environmental accounting into the overall policy milieu. They are preparing case study work in Costa Rica, South Africa, and Indonesia; however this is only one component in their broader environmental work, which spans those working specifically on the environment, those engaged in research, regional and country level work, and EDI's training work. The Bank places environmental accounting within the context of work on economy-environmental linkages, including indicators of environmental progress and world development, research on specific environmental policy problems, country work through the GEF, the national environmental action plans, environmental impact assessments, the country assistance strategies, and so on.

National experience. The experiences with environmental accounting in Namibia and elsewhere in Africa suggest lessons for how to go about implementing integrated accounts. In contrast with some other African projects, the Namibian work has been to a large degree accepted by key government agencies, who are interested in institutionalising environmental accounting within the national accounts process. Several factors in the implementation of the initial pilot project may have contributed to this outcome. The work was part of a comprehensive environmental economics programme launched by the government. This both lowered expectations from any single part of the work and placed it in a broader context which added richness to the results. The effort was clearly internally driven, rather than being imposed upon the government by a donor funding agency. While the lead agency was the Department of Environmental Affairs (Ministry of Environment), which has a mandate for economy-wide environmental activities, the national income accountants were involved throughout as well. This allowed them to feel they were part of the activity without requiring them to put their imprimatur on a new and potentially controversial activity. The focus of the work was consistently on addressing underlying policy questions related to environment-economy linkages, and not on the production of a "green GDP." All of these factors have led to a positive attitude toward the effort, and contributed to Namibia's interest in institutionalising green accounting.

The Chilean experience offers a sharp contrast to Namibia. The work was undertaken by the Central Bank, which prepares the national income accounts. It focused on three sectors (forestry, mining and industry), trying to assess the efficiency and sustainability of the country's resource management strategies. The forestry work, in particular, raised considerable controversy, because the conclusions were that current strategies would not be sustainable and were instead depleting the country's resource base. The project generated substantial public interest, and made environmental accounting into an issue addressed by the political parties. However the Central Bank cut back on its level of effort, apparently at least in part because of the controversial policy implications of the results.

A regional perspective. The European Parliament has voiced significant support for environmental accounting, with physical accounts seen as a first step leading to eventual monetisation in the future. The CEC programme for implementation of the *Direction of the European Union on Environmental Indicators and Green National Accounting* (June 1996) includes a number of elements: (1) measuring the environmental impacts of economic activity; (2) a staged programme of indicators development using the pressure-state-response framework, which will evolve slowly in order to optimise cooperation among EU members; (3) development of an interface to build links between environmental objectives and economic policy; (4) development of satellite accounts which will permit evaluation of the macroeconomic consequences of environmental policy and the environmental impacts of economic policy; (5) in the longer run, multi-criteria analysis of problem pollutants and research on monetised indicators; and (6) other EU projects on economy-environment integration, which should build public awareness of the issues. Germany, in particular, has reacted to this with a fairly high level of support, though the focus is more on the overall process of environmental accounting, rather than specifically on "green GDP" as a single indicator.

Outputs and Follow-up

❑ A base for launching IUCN's green accounting initiative, working at the international, regional, and national levels to support the inclusion of environmental considerations into national accounting; contacts developed across IUCN, with experts in the field, and with regional and national IUCN offices and members interested in learning more and beginning work on environmental accounting. This has provided a solid network of interested people who will participate in the IUCN initiative as it develops.

❑ Workshop report and papers will be placed on the IUCN Economics of Biological Diversity web site by mid-1997.

❑ A more detailed summary, along with copies of the four papers prepared will be available from IUCN-US.

❑ IUCN participation in a joint work plan which includes additional country case studies, training of trainers, policy applications of environmental accounting, and further improvement in methodologies.

Papers and Presentations

1. Introduction to the Issue of SNA Reform and Current National and International Initiatives (Fulai Sheng, WWF International)

2. An Overview Of Current Approaches To Addressing SNA Reform, Including The World Bank's Wealth Of Nations Study (Desmond McCarthy, World Bank)

3. Initiating SNA Reform Processes in Africa, Including a Case Study on Namibia (Glenn-Marie Lange, New York University, USA)

4. A Case Study of the SNA Reform Process and Debates in Chile, with Emphasis on the Forest Sector (Marcel Claude, Chile)

5. Reforming SNA in Europe, an Overview of Current Initiatives and Experiences (Eberhard Seifert, Wuppertal Institute, Germany).

7.6 Structural Adjustment and Conservation

Organizers: National Wildlife Federation; WWF

Chair: Barbara Bramble, NWF

Rapporteurs: Jill Blockhus, Frank Vorhies, IUCN

Summary

Over the past decade the world has witnessed the collapse of socialism and the restructuring of economies in both the "East" and the "South" towards private ownership and freer markets. This restructuring has had both positive and negative impacts on the conservation of nature and natural resources. This workshop focused on the recently- published case studies by WWF which provide insights on how to green structural adjustment programmes. It also included a broad-ranging discussion on the impacts of such programmes on various countries throughout the developing world. A common story is that developing countries have been living beyond their means for too long, and that structural adjustment was necessary.

Objectives

1. To present and review the case studies of WWF.
2. To explore the environmental dimensions of structural adjustment programmes.

Conclusions

A World Bank perspective. The World Bank supports structural adjustment programmes aimed at restoring macro stability, removing distortions from factors such as external trade, internal pricing or regulations, making institutions more efficient, and shifting government focus towards better policy formulation. The World Bank sees a revolution taking place on the role of the state in directing economic policies. As they see it, the role of the state is now moving away from running factories, controlling prices and owning productive resources. It is moving towards setting the rules of the game, supporting health, education and poverty programmes, and focusing on the environment.

Four distinct paths of impact of structural adjustment programmes include (1) relative price shifts, (2) macro stabilisation, (3) institutional adjustment and (4) long-term growth. Each of these paths has good and bad examples of the links between structural adjustment and the environment. The challenge is to follow closely the impacts and potential impacts in order to mitigate those likely to be adverse to the environment.

Relative price shifts focus on liberalising trade by removing subsidies and reducing trade barriers, including currency controls and import duties. A major objective is to make exports more attractive, but this means that the exports of natural resources, such as fish, will also be more attractive. Thus to minimise the impact of liberalising trade on natural resources, such as fish stocks, laws relating to resource access and harvesting, such as fishing laws, need to be reviewed and if necessary revised.

Macro stabilisation focuses on balancing the public budget, which initially means reducing the budget deficit relative to GDP. Two problems must be addressed here. First, a contraction of government spending might cause a contraction in the economy which could put pressure on the environment. Second, for political reasons the contraction of government spending may adversely hit environmental programmes, such as protected areas and forest management rather than reductions in military spending. Thus it is important to monitor closely the possible impacts of macro stabilisation on the environment to make adjustments in the programme when appropriate.

Institutional adjustment focuses on privatisation of government functions better handled by the private sector as well as "corporatisation" of the public sector to improve the efficiency of its operations. Though such adjustments should be good for the environment, they will only be good if the legislation and access rights regarding natural resource utilisation are consistent with the new institutional arrangements.

Finally, long-term economic growth is a mixed blessing with respect to the environment. More growth means more money available for environmental matters, but more growth may also mean more demand for natural resources, such as timber. Again it is important to review the existing legislation and access rights to see if they are consistent with a long-term growth economy.

A WWF perspective. WWF recently completed a 12-country study on the effects of structural adjustment on the environment; the study also took social concerns into account. The broad policy objective of the WWF study was to examine the socio-economic root causes and environmental effects of structural adjustment by trying to: (1) understand the impact on a broad range of countries, mainly extractive and agricultural economies, (2) understand relationships between macroeconomic reforms, poverty, and environment, and (3) assess the impact of adjustment on longer term sustainability of adjusting countries.

A better understanding of the interrelationship between structural adjustment programmes and the environment is necessary if we are going to have truly sustainable development. WWF thus sees its work as supporting efforts to build capacity in local institutions and to build partnerships with development agencies to ensure that environmental considerations are addressed.

The WWF work has led to a number of recommendations for future strategies:

1. Develop transitional strategies to maintain productivity and living standards, including phasing out subsidies to production.

2. Establish a strategic relationship between economic change and environment resources.

3. Identify and strengthen core functions of the State.

4. Strengthen participation of civil society in development and adjustment process.

5. Reform the role of international agencies, in particular by promoting partnerships.

6. Build partnerships with the private sector. Such recommendations make clear the multi-stakeholder approach necessary to ensure that structural adjustment programmes promote efficient, equitable and sustainable development.

Cross-cutting issues

According to the WWF study, costs of structural adjustment have been shouldered by the poor (including women and subsistence farmers). More could be learned about gender if a case study were undertaken on an in-depth analysis of the effects on women and poor segments of society.

Most countries, quite naturally, focus on the challenges of their own structural adjustment programmes. Broader perspectives, such as those of the World Bank and WWF, can help countries review the options before them. Thus more communication is needed about the impacts of structural adjustment programmes on the environment.

Outputs and Follow-up

❏ The workshop report and papers will be placed on the IUCN Economics of Biological Diversity web site by mid-1997.

❏ In the context of structural adjustment programmes, IUCN and its members should create a demand for environmental policy reviews in order to ensure that environmental considerations are not ignored.

❏ Structural adjustment issue are clearly a matter of concern within the IUCN Membership and the Secretariat needs to explore further how to incorporate these issues into its programme of work.

Papers and Presentations

1. The World Bank View of Structural Adjustment (Andrew Steer, Director, Environment Section, The World Bank)

2. The WWF Study on Structural Adjustment and the Environment (Fulai Sheng, WWF International).

3. Panel discussion (Fulai Sheng, WWF), (Lucy Emerton, African Wildlife Foundation), Desmond McCarthy, (the World Bank), and (Arthur Mugisha, Uganda Wildlife Authority).

7.7 Banking on Biodiversity

Organizers: National Wildlife Federation; Friends of the Earth

Chair: Barbara Bramble, NWF, USA

Rapporteurs: Jill Blockhus, Frank Vorhies, IUCN

Summary

UNEP has led an exciting new initiative on banking and the environment. The Global Environment Facility is now moving funds through the International Finance Corporation to finance private sector activities for the environment – including investments in climate change and biodiversity. Interest is growing in trying to redirect private sector capital flows towards biodiversity. This workshop explored the challenges and opportunities of moving private sector money towards conservation objectives.

Objectives

1. To provide an opportunity for the IUCN Membership to explore opportunities for moving private sector funds for biodiversity.

2. To provide inputs into the Investing in Biodiversity workshop planned for the 5th Session of the Global Biodiversity Forum in November 1996 in Buenos Aires scheduled to take place directly before the 3rd meeting of the Conference of the Parties to the Convention on Biological Diversity.

Conclusions

The GEF/IFC SME Programme. The Global Environment Facility (GEF) has been providing relatively small amounts of grant funding to the International Finance Corporation (IFC), the private sector arm of The World Bank Group, in support of biodiversity and climate change activities. Some of this funding has financed the start up of a Small and Medium Enterprise (SME) Programme which makes debt and equity investments in SME activities related to climate change and biodiversity, thus channelling incremental finance to the private sector in developing countries. The SME Programme is an exciting development of turning GEF grant funding into IFC debt/equity financing for biodiversity.

Raising venture capital for biodiversity. Currently very little of the private sector capital flowing to developing countries goes into biodiversity-related investments. Thus conservationists need to identify why biodiversity is not attracting private finance and what incentives need to be developed to change this situation. This would include investigating perverse subsidies (subsidies that work against biodiversity) and other market distortions. Another challenge is to look at greening both consumer demand and investment portfolios. Given the high risk and new directions of biodiversity-relating investments, venture capital financing is probably the right approach. Thus constituencies interested in increasing private sector flows to biodiversity could do well by learning more about venture capital markets.

Emerging enterprise funds should focus on the community. The starting point in most developing countries in not conservation of wildlife, but rather poverty eradication. Thus conservation finance must be linked to improving the quality of life on the ground. For most communities, this means investing in the small and micro enterprises which provide them with both a means of livelihood and necessary goods and services. The key, however, is to set up a structure in which local people are shareholders of investments and not recipients of transfers. Thus developing countries need a community-focused and based enterprise fund which integrates development objectives with conservation objectives. The fund currently being set up in Zimbabwe is one such example.

How the World Bank can help. It is important to put the role of public sector financial institutions into a broader perspective. Annual global production is about $20 trillion of which about 20% or $4 trillion is reinvested. Annual production in the developing world is about $7.5 trillion of which again 20% or $1.5 trillion is reinvested. Some of the reinvestment is from poor farmers without the services of a banking intermediary, but about 66% flows from savers to investors. Of this, about $200 billion annually flows from rich countries to poor countries in the form of private capital, far more than the flows from multilateral financial institutions, such as the World Bank and the UN agencies. The challenge is to ensure that this money stops going to bad projects, but rather is directed to good things, such as biodiversity conservation.

The World Bank has five roles to play:

1. Catalyse private capital flows towards good things, such as its new venture capital funds for biodiversity.

2. Take a piece of the action by guaranteeing a small part of the financing of a business consortium, as it is considering in the electricity sector.

3. Develop acceptable standards for global behaviour of investors, banks, etc.

4. Work with developing countries to create the right atmosphere for environment-friendly investment.

5. Help to strengthen the environment capacity of the banking sector in developing countries.

In all these areas, IUCN could help to promote an interest in exploring ways to increase private sector involvement in biodiversity conservation.

Cross-cutting issues

As many users of biological resources in local and indigenous communities are women, appropriate micro-level financial programmes for on-the-ground conservation cannot be designed without incorporating gender considerations.

Clearly, many things are happening on financial resources for biodiversity. More progress could be made if we could share experiences on specific cases. After finding good examples (particularly on engaging the private sector) we should do our best to get the message across to our members and partners.

Many developing countries have significant legal barriers to private sector investment in biodiversity. These barriers need to be identified and appropriate enabling legislation drafted.

Outputs and Follow-up

❏ The workshop report and papers will be placed on the IUCN Economics of Biological Diversity web site by mid-1997.

❏ Input into the Investing in Biodiversity workshop planned for the 5th Session of the Global Biodiversity Forum in November 1996 in Buenos Aries.

❏ Securing new and additional financial resources for biodiversity will be a priority area of work for IUCN's Biodiversity Programme.

Papers and Presentations

1. The GEF/IFC Small and Medium Enterprise Programme (Doug Salloum, International Finance Corporation)

2. Venture Capital and Biodiversity (J. Steven Lovnick, TransGlobal Ventures, Inc.)

3. A Southern African Emerging Enterprise Fund (Charles Gore, ENDA-ESA Zimbabwe)

4. A World Bank Perspective (Andrew Steer, the World Bank).

8.1 Trade and Sustainable Development

Organizer: National Wildlife Federation, USA

Chair: Ricardo Melendez, International Centre for Trade and Sustainable Development, Switzerland

Rapporteur: Richard Tarasofsky, IUCN Environmental Law Centre

Summary

The subject of international trade and its impact on the environment has become very popular over the past few years. The accelerating pace of trade liberalization, the completion of the Uruguay Round of multilateral trade negotiations and the establishment of the World Trade Organization have all helped focus attention on this major global issue and the threats and opportunities it presents for the environment. While it is clear that the subject is one of importance, it is less clear how the IUCN community should address it. This workshop looked at the links between trade and the environment, and brought them alive through specific case studies, examined the positive and negative impacts of trade on the environment, and reviewed options for IUCN involvement.

Objective

To explore options for IUCN activities in the field of trade and environment.

Conclusions

Trade cuts across all of the issues which concern the environmental community. The "Rio Bargain" is now bankrupt: (a) development aid budgets have been reduced, (b) there has been little progress in the transfer of environmentally-sound technology to the South, and (c) the only part which is left is the prospect of increased access by the South to Northern markets. If UN and World Bank reform do not take place soon, the WTO could become the most powerful international organization.

Trade liberalization has the following *benefits*: a) increased financial resources to invest in environmental protection; b) increased access to efficient environmentally-sound technology; c) learning and norm-building arising from cross-border movement of goods and services; and d) transmission of higher environmental standards through import requirements and best practices of transnational corporations.

The *adverse effects* of trade liberalization arise from the following: a) pressure to compete at any cost; b) inability of commodity producers to pass on price increases triggered by increased costs of environmental measures; and c) pressures from international lenders to boost exports.

The workshop then proceeded to focus on three case studies, designed to highlight particular "trade and environment" problems. First, the ecological harm to important species and ecosystems linked to the production of rice in Uruguay, 90% of which is for export, was examined. Although trade liberalization per se is not to blame for all of this, since environmental harm was also occurring in times of economic protectionism, it is clear that Mercosur imperatives have tended to prevail over conservation ones, leading to the conclusion that in this particular environmental and development context, trade has been harmful.

Second, the adverse environmental effect arise from the heavy use of subsidies in the fishing industry. Efforts to have this highly political issue dealt with at several international fora, including the WTO Committee on Trade and Environment, have so far met with failure. It is only in regional fisheries organizations that change to the rules on subsidies may take place.

The third case study focused on the challenges to sustainable development caused by the structure of the banana market. The focus on this particular commodity brought out the major conflicts between sustainable development and the trade regime in commodity markets – commodities are taken directly from the environment, extraction may have environmental consequences, and people doing the extracting tend to be on the economic fringes of society. Further problems are specific to bananas – principally the inability of the producing countries to capture very much of the economic rent and how this rent can be applied to support sustainable development. Efforts to focus on cost-internalization of environmental harm are misplaced, in that pricing can only be a part of the solution: the key question is whether the right actions are happening, rather than trying to price something to which no true market value can be assigned.

A presentation followed on the regional trade regime created by the North American Free Trade Agreement, the Agreement on Environmental Cooperation and the Commission on Environmental Cooperation. A current complaint before the Commission, regarding Cozumel in Mexico, is a "make or break" case for the Commission in determining its real clout. Although the regime is not perfect, it is a reasonable first step in trying to integrate environmental and trade concerns. Another presentation in the Southern African context highlighted the problems of lack of information and awareness of the linkages between the trade regime and sustainable development. It also revealed that each region has its own particular issues and priorities which set the framework for considering these linkages.

On the debate concerning the environmental costs and benefits of liberalized trade, the issue cannot be examined in a vacuum: what matters most is whether the trade rules are accompanied by sufficiently strong environmental rules. At present, the environmental regime is not sufficiently strong to effectively complement the trade regime. Changes are needed in respect of the following: a) how international trade agreements are negotiated; b) how trade agreements are implemented, c) the rules and culture of trade institutions; and d) how trade institutions relate to other international institutions and other elements of civil society. The theoretical proposition that open markets do a better job of allocating resources more efficiently than closed ones has not been sufficiently empirically tested. There is insufficient hard data on what the environmental impacts of trade liberalization actually are.

As regards developments within the WTO Committee on Trade and Environment (CTE), the current agenda is both too narrow and too unfocused. The flow of information should be altered, including by making the notification requirements of the WTO more effective and more open. Key issues requiring further action are in reconciling the relationship between the TRIPS Agreement and the Convention on Biological Diversity and on accommodating within the trade regime trade measures based on "production and processing methods". The WTO should focus on evaluating whether a measure is protectionist, rather than attempting to make environmental policy determinations. Increased international cooperation between the WTO and other international organizations was considered essential to dealing with these policy issues, especially since the WTO Ministerial Meeting may not yield bold attempts to reform the trading regime, the CTE should not be dismissed by environmentalists: its biggest achievements have been to build confidence among delegations on this issue and the place of "trade and environment" is at the centre of the overall trade policy debate.

Finally, the following current IUCN projects on "trade and environment" were presented for discussion and were welcomed by the participants:

❏ The IISD-IUCN capacity-building initiative

❏ The work of the IUCN Environmental Law Programme

❏ The preparation of a survey on "trade and environment" issues as an awareness building document for IUCN members and other actors

❏ The four-year project on the effective implementation of trade-related aspects of the Convention on Biological Diversity

❏ The International Centre on Trade and Sustainable Development.

Outputs and Follow-up

❏ IUCN's specialist and regional networks should examine and evaluate the environmental impacts of the Uruguay Round.

❏ IUCN will support more empirical work to be done on the environmental impacts of trade liberalization.

❏ IUCN will support defining an appropriate relationship between IPRs and the Convention on Biological Diversity.

Papers and Presentations

1. What is the Relationship between Trade and Environment, and Why is it Important? (James Cameron, Foundation for International Environmental Law and Development)

2. Bananas (Konrad von Moltke, IISD)

3. Rice and Wetlands (Eduardo Gudynas, CLAES)

4. Fisheries and Subsidies (Cliff Curtis, Greenpeace)

5. How Trade Liberalization can Benefit Environmental Protection (Simon Tay, National University of Singapore)

6. How Trade Liberalization can Harm Environmental Protection (Charles Arden-Clarke, WWF-Int)

7. The Environmental Agenda of WTO: Accomplishments and Predictions (Scott Vaughan, WTO and Brennan Van Dyke, CIEL)

8. A Southern View on Trade Negotiations (Diana Tussie, FLACSO/IDCTSD, and Aaron Crosbey, IISD).

David Runnalls, IISD Canada
Eduardo Gudyñas, CLAES, Uruguay
Cliff Curtis, Greenpeace, USA
Konrad von Moltke, WWF-US
Pierre-Marc Johnson, Canada
Charles Arden-Clarke, WWF International, Switzerland
Scott Vaughan, WTO, Switzerland
Nakatiwa Mulikita, ZERO, Zimbabwe
Aaron Cosbey, IISD, Canada
Nicholas Robinson, Pace University, USA
Richard Tarasofsky, IUCN-ELC, Germany

8.2 International Forest Policy Processes

Organizer: IUCN and the International Institute for Sustainable Development (IISD)

Chair: Angela Cropper, United Nations Development Programme (UNDP)

Rapporteur: Mark Dillenbeck, IUCN-US

Summary

The world is filled with unparalleled risks and opportunities as we face the greatest growth in population and technological advances in history. Forests provide a test case of whether we can develop sustainably and the challenge of sustainable forest management is primarily political rather than technical. At the time of the WCC, the most ambitious and far-reaching discussions on forest conservation and sustainable development were well underway around the globe. The Intergovernmental Panel on Forests (IPF) had just completed its penultimate session, and the World Commission on Forests and Sustainable Development (WCFSD) had just held the second of five planned Regional Public Hearings. In international political fora the shift in emphasis from tropical forests to all forests has helped to further progress by putting all players on a more equal footing. The shift has also helped to illuminate problems in boreal and temperate zones which had previously been obscured by the focus on the tropics.

Objectives

1. To review expected outputs from the international dialogue on forests.

2. To discuss possible future options.

3. To recommend policy priorities for IUCN.

Conclusions

The international forest policy processes (Intergovernmental Panel on Forests, World Commission on Forests and Sustainable Development and the Convention on Biological Diversity) have increased the political attention placed on forests and this is a necessary prerequisite for action. Unfortunately, the positive rhetoric of the international discussions has not been complemented by actions on the ground. Outputs have been very limited and this has led to increased frustration from many participants, particularly NGOs.

On the positive side of the ledger, the international forest policy processes (a) have helped generate a greater commitment to the definition and implementation of criteria and indicators for sustainable forest management, (b) are likely to lead to improvements in the conduct of the Global Forest Resource Assessment, (c) have generated interest and support for National Forest Plans, and (d) have helped raise awareness of indigenous people's issues.

Other major conclusions included:

❑ International policy dialogues have a big influence on less-developed country national policy development. This is not fully appreciated by NGOs and developed countries.

❑ The international forest policy processes are providing needed external pressure for change.

❑ Global needs (e.g. biodiversity conservation, carbon sequestration) need to be reconciled with national sovereignty.

❑ The lack of political will at the national level is a major problem which can be addressed by developing a civil society constituency for forest conservation.

❑ Many of the real causes of deforestation are not being addressed by inter-governmental processes (e.g. land tenure, corruption, lack of incentives, lack of political will, etc.). The comparative advantage of the WCFSD is that it is able to address some of the more controversial issues.

❑ Existing agreements and instruments are being held up by the IPF dialogue (e.g. CBD with respect to forests).

❑ Continuance of the IPF and/or pursuit of a global forest convention could distract from implementation of existing agreements and other concrete actions. Talk is expensive.

❑ Future forest dialogues could separate the scientific from the political discussions, perhaps following the model of the Intergovernmental Panel on Climate Change.

❑ Regional agreements may be more promising since the players are likely to have more in common.

❑ Independent processes (e.g. Forest Stewardship Council) may yield better results.

❑ Workshop participants were divided on the need for a forest convention.

Outputs and Follow-up

IUCN will seek to:

❑ Play the role of expert advisor to the IPF follow-up process. This might be a role that would be similar to that played by IUCN in the CITES context.

❑ Assist the CBD COP in defining a framework for action on forests and to identify and pursue research priorities through SBSTTA.

❑ Provide a fora for discussions on issues which are not on the international agenda such as underlying causes of deforestation, land tenure, unsustainable consumption, etc.

❑ Promote partnerships between government, NGOs and the private sector and in particular, IUCN could do much more to influence the private sector.

❏ Help to develop and implement criteria and indicators, especially C&I for measuring forest health.

❏ Support and evaluate the implementation of existing international mechanisms for sustainable forest management.

Papers and Presentations

1. Manuel Rodriguez, Co-chair, Intergovernmental Panel on Forests (IPF)

2. Ola Ullsten, Co-Chair, World Commission on Forests and Sustainable Development (WCFSD)

3. Jean-Pierre Martel, Director of Forest Policy, Canadian Pulp and Paper Association

4. Bill Mankin, Director, Global Forest Policy Project

5. David Cassels, Environmental Specialist, World Bank.

8.3 The Future of Development Cooperation

Organizer: International Institute for Environment and Development (IIED)

Chair: David Runnalls, International Institute for Sustainable Development, Canada

Rapporteur: Aaron Cosbey

Summary

At the Earth Summit in 1992, the aid-giving countries committed themselves to make renewed efforts to attain the goal – established in 1966 – of providing 0.7% of GNP in development assistance. Despite that, both the total volume of aid, and the proportion of GNP devoted to aid, have been in retreat ever since and are now at the lowest level – in real terms – since the early 1970s. This tendency could be dangerous for conservation, with an increasing proportion of conservation activity in the developing countries dependent on development aid funding. This workshop explored the trends, the reasons for them, what might be done to redefine, refocus, and improve the delivery of development assistance, and the strategies that might be followed to generate more political support for aid budgets.

Objectives

1. To explore recent trends in official development assistance in general, and funding for biodiversity conservation in particular.

2. To explore the reasons underlying downturns in aid funding, and to assess their significance in terms of conservation.

3. To identify elements critical to conservation that must be retained in the overall aid frame.

4. To agree on approaches and actions to refocus aid in favour of the environment, and to lobby for a renewed commitment to aid allocations in national budgets.

Conclusions

The six speakers in this workshop began with consensus on a body of assumptions. The OECD aid frame is in decline, and will continue to be in the foreseeable future. It is often claimed that the failure of this element of the "Rio bargain" is offset by a commensurate rise in the flows of foreign direct investment (FDI), but the vast majority of FDI is directed at a handful of relatively well-off countries, and cannot be considered a substitute for well-structured official development assistance (ODA).

As the workshop progressed, consensus was reached as well on the nature of the crisis in ODA, centring on three themes:

❏ OECD countries, with the end of the cold war, have lost sight of the strategic rationale for ODA. There is no recognition of the role ODA can play in assuring common security, and no apparent recognition of the moral imperative to narrow the widening North-South gaps in development.

❏ ODA has not traditionally done enough to foster real development. It has been based on discrete short-term projects, rather than ongoing programmes, and thus rather than building institutions or capacity may in fact create debilitating dependencies. Long-term disbursement mechanisms such as trust funds were noted as alternatives, as were flows based on such sources as global tradable emissions schemes and protection of biodiversity.

❏ Neither has traditional ODA done enough to protect the environment – a key element in the well-being of current and future generations. This current squeeze in funding will only make this worse.

IUCN is increasingly broadening its focus from the environmental effects of economic processes to also examine the underlying dynamics which drive those processes. The nature and future of DA clearly falls into this category of meta-themes. One speaker proposed that the IUCN membership should address the issues in a series of regional debates – a process which would benefit both the membership and the efforts to redesign the current practice of ODA.

Another speaker focused particularly on the problems of declining *quality* of ODA, accompanying and precipitated to some degree by the decline in *quantity* discussed above. While the demand, with our increasing understanding of the nature of social and environmental development, is for labour-intensive small-scale disbursements, this runs up against the reality of staff cuts. The EU, for example, has one environmental officer per $1.3 billion disbursed, vs. one per $118,000 in the World Bank. The result is an inefficient end-of-pipe approach to environment in the aid framework. A general result is a vicious cycle of declining effectiveness, deteriorating public image, and further decreased flows.

The trends in ODA for NGOs. For a number of reasons, OECD governments over the last decade have directed an increasing share of ODA through NGOs. But NGOs have traditionally served *two* important roles; not only have they been disbursement media, but they have also been forces for social change, agitating and educating to alter the systematic problems which give rise to the need for ODA and environmental activism in the first place. NGOs increasingly dependent on government aid contracts may not be able to fulfil this latter role adequately, at a time when the need is increasing for voices in the North on issues such as consumption, and the nature of real development.

New delivery mechanisms. The primary goal is poverty alleviation, and ODA is an investment which plays a *complementary* role in this process, aiding appropriate domestic policies, and acting in partnership with other countries and NGOs. A new paradigm for aid needs to strive for economic growth and private sector co-operation, greater respect for the environment, and a stronger involvement of women. Donors need to act only where they can identify their comparative advantage, to focus on programmes rather than projects, and to measure quality in terms of results rather than by quantity of funds disbursed.

Development assistance has costs. As traditionally conceived, aid has social and environmental costs which may outweigh its benefits. Like subsidies, aid has created dependency in its recipients, destroying the innovative spirit necessary for development. As well, since aid tends to go to safe, convenient sponsors (governments), and focus on short projects (3–4 years), it has resulted in little real building of capacity or institutions. Not only does aid need to be fundamentally redesigned, but new sources of funding should be sought by the South, focusing not on FDI and neo-liberal reforms, but on flows which acknowledge the role of the South in such areas as preserving biodiversity, and on global schemes for carbon-emission and ozone depletion rights.

ODA, because it is unpredictable in extent and duration, tends to create an extroversion in its recipients; each looks to the next higher level outward for solutions to its problems, ending with national governments looking to agencies such as the World Bank and to bilateral donors. Development thinking has evolved, broadening the focus from physical capital, to include human capital, natural capital and now social capital; how does ODA contribute to the building of the social institutions that underlie a society's capacity to provide for human needs. One answer is that it does not – that by its creation of extroversion it in fact destroys such capacity. New sources of funding based on the global environmental services provided by the South would appear to be a productive solution.

Outputs and Follow-up

❑ IUCN should help ODA agencies to adjust to the new more market-based macroeconomic development policies which the North is implementing globally while preserving aid for the social and environmental priorities which the market does not adequately address.

❑ IUCN should emphasize increasing global interdependence as a way to help overcome donor fatigue.

❑ IUCN should promote the idea of predictable, automatic ODA funding on schemes such as carbon permits or fees on civil aviation, international financial transactions, or other trade-related criteria, with the purpose to replace charities with entitlements for disadvantaged countries and regions, and to support sustainable development objectives at the same time.

Papers and Presentations

1. Introduction and the Challenge (Richard Sandbrook, IIED)

2. The Record to Date on Biodiversity (Rob Lake, RSPB)

3. The Overall Record with NGOs and Civil Society (Ian Smillie, IDRC)

4. Aid in Practice, and its Limits (David Hales, USAID)

5. Aid? Forget it! (Ashok Khosla, Development Alternatives)

6. Redefining the Agenda (Tariq Banuri, SDPI).

8.4 Rio+5 Consultations

Organizer: The Earth Council

Chairs: Maximo Kalaw and Mahbubul Haq, The Earth Council

Rapporteur: Urs Thomas

Summary

More than a workshop, this was an information session on the cycle of events being organized to review the implementation of the Rio Declaration, Agenda 21, and the other commitments made at the UN Conference on Environment and Development in 1992. A special focus was placed on the process for developing an Earth Charter, one of the main initiatives of The Earth Council.

Objectives

1. To brief the IUCN constituency on plans to review the results of Rio five years on.

2. To inform them of opportunities for involvement in both the governmental and NGO cycles of meetings and events.

3. To highlight the process for developing the Earth Charter.

Conclusions

The programme of events must not be used solely to review the achievements of five years of effort following the Earth Summit, but more important to address and understand both the successes and failures and the reasons for them, to revitalize commitment to implement Agenda 21, and to address issues neglected at Rio.

The Earth Charter process, which has its origins in the report of the Brundtland Commission in 1987, aims to go beyond the Rio Declaration and heighten the consensus around the goal of sustainable development. The broad and open process leading to its adoption is a particularly good opportunity for the IUCN constituency.

Outputs and Follow-up

Recommendations for IUCN:

❏ In view of widespread conference fatigue, do not recycle the same old resolutions again

❑ Focus on operational strategies and follow-up structures, i.e., a multi-stakeholder process, including Business Councils, churches, etc.

❑ Participate in the integrative workshops on institutions, policy and finance.

❑ Elaborate a position on the controversy over the question whether individual species should be emphasized or only general principles like concerns over the abuse and cruelty to animals (international law has never addressed the intrinsic value of species).

Papers and Presentations

1. Briefing on the Official UN Review Process for 1997 (Zehra Aydin, UN Department of Policy Coordination and Sustainable Development)

2. Briefing on the Independent Review Process for 1997 (Maximo Kalaw, Executive Director, The Earth Council)

3. Briefing on the Earth Charter Process (Steven Rockefeller, Middlebury College)

4. The IUCN Ethics Working Group and the Earth Charter (J. Ronald Engel, Ethics Working Group, IUCN Commission on Environmental Strategy and Planning)

5. Discussant (Ambassador Mohamed Sahnoun, The Earth Council).

8.5 Environment and Security

Organizer: IUCN

Chair: Ghaith H. Fariz, The Azraq Oasis Conservation Project, Jordan

Rapporteur: Urs Thomas

Summary

The link between environment and security has attracted a great deal of attention in recent years. For one thing, the relationship between environmental degradation and the displacement of peoples is being studied closely, as is the relationship between such degradation and conflict. At the same time, these links appear to offer new ways of attracting political attention to the environment, and further support to environmental action. Yet the field is young. There remain a number of different schools of thought on the topic, and much groundwork is still to be done before the arguments can really be made compelling. The notion of security, for example, varies from place to place, with definitions running from the restricted military notions of national security, to broader definitions of the security of people and communities. The quantitative evidence for the relations between resource scarcity and conflict, too, remain tenuous.

Objectives

1. To explore perspectives on the subject from North and South.

2. To examine a number of specific case studies aimed at bringing the issues into sharper focus.

3. To identify a role for IUCN in this emerging field.

Conclusions

Environment and Security is not a new programme area for IUCN, nor does attention to it require any amendment to the mission statement. Instead, IUCN should pay closer attention to the security dimension of much of its work in the field, and take full advantage of the linkages to reinforce the argument for environmental action. Particular attention should be paid to the potential for environmental action to prevent or mitigate conflict, and the involuntary displacement of peoples.

Outputs and Follow-up

IUCN should:

❑ identify ES danger zones with the objective of providing counsel, preventive diplomacy, serving as an "honest broker", perhaps in conjunction with other organizations such as OAU;

❏ publicise success stories, e.g., the white rhino, extirpated from Chad, Sudan, and Uganda, with only 11 left in Zaire in 1985, increased to 33 in 1995 thanks to cooperation between IUCN, WWF and the Zoological Society of Frankfurt;

❏ cooperate with the UNHCR on refugee settlements, with UNESCO-MAB on more flexible buffer zones of biosphere reserves, with the International Law Commission on environmental regimes (e.g., on development of water basins);

❏ contribute to the assessment of scientific evaluation methods for environment and security.

Papers and Presentations

Presentations were made by:

1. Mapping out the Field: Overview (Günther Bachler, Swiss Peace Foundation)

2. Simmons, Environmental Change and Security Project, Smithsonian Institution: Overview

3. José Happart, European Parliament

4. Lennart Olsson, European Parliament

5. Alec Watson, The Nature Conservancy, USA

6. Oleg Kolbasov, Institute of State and Law, Moscow, Russia

7. Eduardo Fernandez, IUCN-US

8. Hasna Moudud, NARI, Dhaka, Bangladesh: Inland Waters

9. Karl Hansen, IISD, Canada: Forests

10. Michael Brklacich, Carleton University, Ottawa, Canada: Mapping areas of risk.

9.1 Managing for Sustainability in Canada's Arctic: Valuing Time-Honored Traditions and Resolving Modern Environmental Issues

Organizers: Terry Fenge, Canadian Arctic Resources Committee
Mark Graham, Canadian Museum of Nature
Albert Haller, Canadian Polar Commission
Gisèle Jacob, Mining Association of Canada
Fred McFarland, Indian and Northern Affairs Canada
Fred Roots, Environment Canada
The Steering Committee for Workshops on the Arctic
The Canadian Polar Commission

Chairs: Mark Graham, Canadian Museum of Nature; Whit Fraser, Canadian Polar Commission

Rapporteur: Fred Roots

Summary

This workshop included a set of self-contained sessions, interlinked in a logical thematic suite. The first session presented concrete examples of research and application of traditional knowledge, and of current innovative and successful participatory approaches in wildlife management and mine development and operation. In the second session, a panel focused specifically on the presence and transport of contaminants into Arctic ecosystems, perhaps the most complex and challenging issue that Arctic Peoples must confront, concluding with a wrap-up panel discussion involving a range of key players in the Arctic. This panel interacted with all participants to bring out the highlights of the day, and to identify how IUCN, and other leading national and international NGOs and agencies, can contribute more to meeting the environmental challenges of the Arctic. One of the key aspects in this workshop was the extensive participation of representatives of the Aboriginal peoples of the Arctic, as presenters and resource people.

Objectives

1. To allow for representatives of Aboriginal Peoples, and for other players in the Arctic, to outline and discuss actual cases pertaining to the sustainable use of renewable and of non-renewable resources in the Arctic, and to focus on the major challenges – environmental and socioeconomic – which must be addressed.

2. To draw on the results of a conference on contaminants held in Iqaluit, Northwest Territories, immediately prior to the World Conservation Congress, in order to identify what can be done to help Arctic Peoples confront this major issue for achieving a sustainable future.

Conclusions

The issue of borne contaminants in the Arctic must be addressed with great urgency. Some indigenous groups are exposed to levels of contaminants in excess of tolerable intake. In the case of PCBs and pesticides, for example, levels in newborns have been found to be anywhere from two to ten times higher than those recorded in southern regions. Arctic peoples are also exposed to higher levels of heavy metals (e.g., cadmium, mercury) and radionuclides than are populations in the South. While measures to reduce or eliminate the use of such substances have lowered the exposure risk to some degree, researchers suggest that long-lived contaminants will continue to be recycled within regional ecosystems for many years to come.

The Arctic is under attack and must be defended in the short term because: a) of the acute pervasive effect of the borne contaminants on the health of the ecosystems (and on humans as the last echelon in the food chain – the Arctic people depend on wildlife, now contaminated, for their living); and b) of the fragility of the Arctic and of its inability to restore itself rapidly. Participants called on IUCN to apply the Union's leverage to promote international pressure for saving and decontaminating the Arctic.

Aboriginal peoples do not reject development. They welcome development, but on the conditions that: a) they be true partners for planning and applying the development initiatives; b) the financial return be equitably shared; and c) appropriate balance be found between the unavoidable detrimental effects and the desirable benefits for the community.

Participatory management is feasible and may well ensure achieving this fragile balance. This has been well demonstrated by the case study of the Raglan Mine in Northern Québec.

Certain conditions are key to effective participatory management. The leading players must be truly dedicated and willing to spend the resources that the process requires, and the results of negotiations ideally must be formalized in a binding document. Imposing formal regulatory or convention frameworks, or strong government stewardship, can provide the supportive environment required for all parties to enter into serious discussions.

Where sustainable use/development in traditional communities is concerned, traditional knowledge plays an essential role. It can provide some key data required for decision making, create the right cultural context, and foster the mutual confidence required for creative and constructive debates. Traditional knowledge cannot be used or considered out of its cultural context. Therefore, the holders of the knowledge must be intimately involved in its use and control.

Traditional knowledge is being lost. Means of passing on the knowledge from the elders to the younger generation must be found, in order to: a) preserve the culture of the aboriginal peoples, and b) to ensure the appropriate collection and the dynamic preservation of this knowledge. One cannot acknowledge the great importance of traditional knowledge, for the sustainable development of the populated areas and for effective participatory management, without acknowledging in the same breath that the holders of such knowledge are disappearing fast. In this respect, to quote a presenter, "Traditional knowledge should be on the list of endangered species".

Cross-cutting issues

Many of the presenters were women, who play a significant role in leading aboriginal organizations in Canada, and often are the key holders of many components of traditional knowledge. With regard to borne contaminants, women are particularly concerned and have a notable word to say because when affected by contaminants, they transmit these to their offspring through maternal blood and breast feeding.

One of the main reasons for the rapid loss of traditional knowledge is that most of it is transmitted through oral communication, and thus disappears with the holders. Effective means of collecting the tradition must be designed and applied urgently. With regard to participatory management, respectful two-way communication is essential between the parties, and can only be achieved if the right degree of mutual confidence is reached.

Imposing formal regulatory or convention frameworks sets the right context for all parties to enter into serious discussions where participatory management is desirable. With regard to traditional knowledge, participants once again insisted that much needs to be done, and little has been done, to enshrine in some formal way the legitimacy of traditional knowledge and the related intellectual rights.

Outputs and Follow-up

❑ A recommendation to IUCN to "**apply the Union's leverage to promote international pressure for saving and decontaminating the Arctic**".

❑ The organizers of the Arctic Workshop dedicated this day to the late Honorable Jim Bourque, a prominent aboriginal political and social figure in the Arctic. Jim made the opening comment for the Closing Panel. He passed away in Ottawa, two days later.

Papers and Presentations

1. Opening remarks (Mark Graham, Director of Research, Canadian Museum of Nature)

2. Sustainability in the Arctic: An overview of Arctic Issues and Opportunities from an Aboriginal Perspective (Mary Simon, Canadian Ambassador for Circumpolar Affairs, IUCN Councillor)

3. Research and Application of Traditional Knowledge: Introduction (Terry Fenge, Canadian Arctic resources Committee)

4. Case Study: The Hudson Bay Programme: Traditional Ecological Knowledge Research (Peter Kattuk, Zak Novalinga, Miriam McDonald, Luke Arragutainaq, Environmental Committee of Sanikiluak)

5. Participatory Management and Use of Renewable Resources (Fred MacFarland, Indian and Northern Affairs, Canada)

6. Case Study: The Inuvialuit Settlement Region (Larry Carpenter, Duane Smith and Billy Day, Inuvialuit Game Council)

7. The Raglan Mine in Northern Quebec (Hans Matthews, Canadian Aboriginal Minerals Association. Presentations by Thomas F. Pugsley, Falconbridge Ltd., Robert Lanarie, Makivik Corporation, Willie Kitanic, Mayor of Salluit and Robbie Keith, Environmentalist)

8. Contaminants in Arctic Ecosystems: Changing the Sustainability Equation (Whit Fraser, Canadian Polar Commission)

9. Contaminants in the Arctic: Sources and Trends: A Scientific Overview (John Stager, Canadian Polar Commission)

10. Contaminants in the Arctic: Risks and Realities: A View from the Communities (Aboriginal representatives)

11. Arctic Day Closing Panel: Highlights of the day and focus for recommendations (Hon. Jim Bourque, Centre of Traditional Knowledge, Fred Roots, Science Advisor Emeritus, Environment Canada; Joanne Barnaby, Dene Cultural Institute; Ambassador Mary Simon).

9.2 Plannning and Establishing a Protected Areas System

Organizer: Neil Munro, Parks Canada

Chair: Neil Munro, Parks Canada

Rapporteur: Kevin McNamee, Canadian Federation of Nature

Summary

In response to the direction proposed by the WCED (Our Common Future, 1987), Canada and its provinces have signed a commitment to complete Canada's networks of protected areas representative of the country's land-based natural regions by the year 2000, and accelerate the protection of areas representative of Canada's marine natural regions. Over the years, excellent models of system planning have been developed at both national and provincial levels as a base for guiding the achievement of this goal. During the workshop on system planning, a global overview presentation was followed by specific presentations, with comments by a panel at the end. The members of the panel have demonstrated the relevance of the examples given, noted opportunities for improvement, and highlighted approaches and ideas that could be useful elsewhere.

Objectives

1. To provide a contemporary yet futuristic overview of Canadian practices and experience in protected areas system planning, that other countries may wish to emulate.

2. To provide a summary of management issues and challenges facing system planning, both at national and at territorial/provincial levels.

Conclusions

Strategic planning is an essential tool for charting effective sustainable development at reasonable cost. System planning is a must for the establishment of protected areas, with due consideration for the broader political, economic, social and environmental context in which they will be administered once established. The future challenges include the need to manage these new areas, and to take further action to complete the system plans, in a time of constrained budgets.

The creation of protected areas must be part of a broader regional approach to protecting the entire landscape, and action must be taken to ensure that adjacent lands are managed to ensure their ecological integrity.

Aboriginal people and the communities that will be affected by the creation of new protected

areas must be directly involved in planning, evaluating and negotiating the impact and benefits of new protected areas. However, patience is necessary because it can take years to achieve the required level of cooperation.

The objectives and rationale for protected areas system planning must be both established and clearly communicated to the public and decision makers, and should be designed to ensure that both social and conservation goals are adequately addressed.

Cross-cutting issues

People recognize the value of protected areas as dramatic and inspiring landscapes that support recreation. However, given the important role of protected areas in protecting biodiversity, it is important to undertake a broad based communications effort to explain to the public the ecological benefits of those areas, particularly to adjacent landowners and communities, to ensure the ecological integrity of both protected areas and surrounding lands and waters.

The ratification of constitutionally-enshrined land claim agreements between governments and aboriginal people can provide a strong legal mechanism for pursuing the protection of the environment and the establishment of new protected areas. Such agreements provide the legal basis for the direct involvement of aboriginal people in co-managing the environment, and in particular wildlife and protected areas. These agreements also provide more detailed interpretation of general provisions in legislation that guarantee the right of aboriginal people to hunt, trap and fish in national parks within conservation goals.

Outputs and Follow-up

Because this workshop had a demonstration purpose, presentations and discussions have led to conclusions, as outlined above. There have been no formal recommendations or commitments to a formal output.

Papers and Presentations

1. Introduction: An Global Overview (Neil Munro on behalf of Adrian Davey, WCPA).

2. The BC Experience (Derek Thompson, Land Use Coordination Office, Province of British Columbia)

3. A Systems Plan For Nova Scotia (Barry Diamond, Parks, Province of Nova Scotia)

4. New National Parks and National Marine Conservation Areas in Canada (Murray McComb, Parks Canada)

5. A View from the North (Peter Green, Paolatuk, NWT)

6. Advocating and Evaluating Success (Natalie Zinger, WWF-Canada)

7. A Student View (Karen Beazley, Dalhousie University)

8. Comments Relating to Tanzania's Experience in Protected Areas Systems Planning (Lota Melamari, Tanzania National Parks).

9.3 Developing a Business Approach to Protected Areas Management

Organizer: Neil Munro, Parks Canada

Chair: Tony Bull, Parks Canada

Rapporteur: John Cartwright, University of Western Ontario

Summary

In light of the significant reduction in the funding of government programmes, protected area management agencies are seeking alternative means of cost reduction, revenue generation and programme delivery, while maintaining high quality client service and protection of the natural and cultural resources the organizations are mandated to protect. Following an overview introduction at the opening of the workshop, selected presentations focused on approaches that have been tried, or that are under development, for adopting a more business-oriented approach to the management and operation of protected areas. Comments by panel members followed.

Objectives

1. To provide a contemporary yet futuristic overview of Canadian and USA practices and experience for funding protected areas under increasingly severe budget constraints, that other countries may wish to take inspiration from.

2. To expose and discuss management issues and challenges with the commercialization of aspects of protected area operations.

Conclusions

Serious reductions in government spending are a fact of life, and as a consequence consideration must be given to innovative and even controversial approaches to resourcing protected areas, including forms of privatization, market pricing and partnership.

However, governments should not be "left off the hook". Parks are a public benefit and should be paid for at least in part with public money.

One key side effect of budget limitations is that government agencies have been forced to review their mandates and commitments, and to refocus and clarify their priorities. The essential goal of preserving ecological integrity must remain, while significant consideration is given to providing the public with recreational and other opportunities to appreciate parks, from which revenue can be generated. However, a business approach can be risky because there may be too much emphasis on things that have a monetary value, as opposed to those that have no such value.

Outputs and Follow-up

Because this workshop had a demonstration purpose, presentations and discussions have led to conclusions only, as outlined above. There have been no formal recommendations or commitments to a formal output.

Papers and Presentations

1. The Parks Canada Business Plan: Towards a Separate Services Agency (Pat Borbey, Parks Canada Investments)

2. Clarifying and Focusing on the Mandate (Bruce Duffin, Parks Management Support, Province of Alberta)

3. The New Management Equation (Luc Berthiaume, Recreation and Parks, Province of Quebec)

4. The New Agenda (Norm Richards, Ontario Parks)

5. South African National Park: Another View (Robbie Robinson, National Parks Board of South Africa)

6. Pay As You Go: The American Experience? (Randal O'Toole, Thoreau Institute, Oregon)

7. A Business Viewpoint (Jean-Michel Perron, Kilometres Voyages Inc.)

8. An Environmentalist Viewpoint: Who Will Survive, the Beggars or the Bears? (Kevin McNamee, Canadian Nature Federation)

9. An Academic Viewpoint (Robert Payne, Lakehead University).

9.4 Interlinking the Economy, the Communities, and the Environment, for Integrated Land Use Planning and Energy Policy at Government Level

Organizer: Antoine Leclerc, on behalf of the Canadian Committee of IUCN

Chair: Alan Emery, President of the Canadian Committee of IUCN

Rapporteur: Alan Emery

Summary

Two presentations reviewed: a) the factors leading to the need for a new comprehensive land use plan for the Province of British Columbia, and the linkages, successes and failures of the Province's new land use planning policies, programmes and initiatives; and, b) the vast government consultation of the Province of Québec stakeholders for energy development and use, with focus on the factors leading to the need for an energy policy in Québec, and on the process and results of extensive public participation. A critical examination was made of how well the provincial governments achieved their stated goals through these processes.

Objectives

1. To enable the participants to learn from two unique Canadian initiatives for strategic land use and energy policy, which involved in-depth public participation.

2. To discuss the concept and the methods applied elsewhere.

3. To retain ideas that could be applied elsewhere.

Conclusions

Reaching consensus among potentially competing parties, and building on the consensus rather than continued confrontation, can result in a very powerful instrument to influence public policy, laws and regulations for sustainable use. This approach to multi-stakeholder participation in the development and application of sustainable development policies achieves buy-in and support. In this context, new policies tend to be applied sooner and at a lower cost because of this consultation and of the resulting commitments by all parties.

Economic development and support are key to the success of navigating from one state of management and culture to another, in the use of land and natural resources. Here again, broad-based buy-in can be a key factor, where it allows the fiscal burden to be spread thinner because of an increased number of stakeholders. This can contribute to alleviate the feeling that sustainable use is "costly" and the burden inequitably shared.

Economic development can be achieved without increasing the need for energy, given the right context and framework. Where the economy is a prime concern, no development is not the solution.

Because sustainable development can be an all-inclusive concept, that can mean sustaining jobs as well as the natural environment, there is a need to define targets first in order to ensure that measurement of performance is clear and easily communicated. In this context, extensive public consultation can lead to consensus and to acceptable solutions even where extensive societal and environmental issues appear insurmountable.

Cross-cutting issues

Communications were at the root of the success for both case studies. Despite the emphasis on other issues, it was obvious to the listener that one of the key factors for success was clear communication. The approach invited influential input from stakeholders, and ensured that people understood the process, the results and their expected impact.

Law was one of the instruments for locking in the results of the consultative processes. This implies that the willingness of government decision-making bodies to proceed with conclusive legal and regulatory frameworks is an important facet of these consultative and consensus based successes.

Outputs and Follow-up

Because this workshop had a demonstration purpose, presentations and discussions have led to conclusions only, as outlined above. There have been no formal recommendations or commitments to a formal output.

Papers and Presentations

1. Delivering Land Use Planning in British Columbia (Warren Mitchell, Derek Thompson and Karen Lewis, British Columbia Land Use Coordination Office and Dennis O'Gorman, Louise Goulet and Ken Morrison, British Columbia Parks)

2. Towards a Quebec Policy for the Sustainable Use of Energy (Alban D'Amours, Président de la table de consultation, secrétariat du débat sur l'energie du Québec).

9.5 Planning Specific Areas for Sustainable Use

Organizer: Man and the Biosphere Committee for Canada and the Canadian Forest Service

Chair: Jacques Prescott, Secretary of the Canadian Committee of IUCN

Rapporteur: Terence Cooke, MAB Canada, and Miel Corbett, Author

Summary

A combination of two self-contained demonstration sessions gave practical examples of initiatives to integrate conservation and use within specific multiple-use areas. The first, from a forest sector perspective, described and illustrated novel approaches currently applied in Canada to achieve sustainable forestry: model forests, codes of practices, and other voluntary forest initiatives. The second, from a broader conservation perspective, described and illustrated successes and challenges of community-based sustainable development areas. Focus for both sessions was on practical examples where all parties work together voluntarily towards integrating different needs, visions and perspectives, with a definite goal for conservation and full consideration for an overlay of socio-economic factors.

Objectives

1. To provide the participants with practical illustrations of action oriented, living laboratories, that demonstrate the value of integrated resource management and decision making.

2. To demonstrate readiness in Canada and other countries and to call for cooperation for developing mechanisms to exchange and optimize knowledge between communities and stakeholders, and to encourage more communities and stakeholders to participate in the establishment of sustainable development areas.

Conclusions

The people were ahead of the government and industry in understanding the complexity of forest issues, and in the development of the changes which resulted in the establishment of the model forest programme.

The model forest and sustainable development area approaches are already producing useful results for sustainable use/development. The lessons learned provide a foundation for developing parameters which can assist communities to advance their successes, and set a framework and criteria to guide new community initiatives.

Industry participation in model forests is meaningful and not just window dressing. In Canada and other countries, there is a beginning of participation of the private sector in a sincere effort to face the challenge of sustainability, and it must be accounted for.

Both model forests and other sustainable development areas such as UNESCO Biosphere Reserves, require formal criteria and decentralized frameworks, strongly supported by governments, industry and other local stakeholders. Wherever and for whatever reasons these multi-stakeholder community-based processes have been implemented, there are numerous examples that demonstrate the unique contribution and cost effectiveness of these approaches in implementing sustainable development and biodiversity conservation.

These approaches challenge governments, the private sector and other local organizations to cooperate in new ways, which may not yet be widely accepted or understood but which are already producing dividends for those involved.

Cross-cutting issues

Because fully functioning sustainable development areas require by definition the participation of all local stakeholders, they provide *inter alia* new avenues to address gender issues.

Communications between sustainable development areas as well as stakeholders should be given the highest priority.

It is timely to explore the potential for legislation to support more specifically sustainable development initiatives.

Outputs and Follow-up

Because this workshop had a demonstration purpose, presentations and discussions have led to conclusions only, as outlined above. There have been no formal recommendations or commitments to a formal output.

Papers and Presentations

1. Perspectives and Thrust on Sustainable Use in Forestry (Yvan Hardy, Canadian Forest Service)
2. Developing Practical Tools for Sustainable Forest Management (Bob Udell)
3. Aboriginal Participation in the Canadian Forest Sector in the '90s (Peggy Smith)
4. Integrating Biodiversity Values in Operational Forestry (Shane Mahoney)
5. L'approche québécoise à la gestion des forêts conformément aux principes du développement durable (Marc Ledoux)
6. Approaches to Canadian Sustainable Development Areas (David Neave, Wildlife Habitat Canada)
7. An Overview of Canadian Sustainable Development Area Activity (Terence Cook, Coordinator, Canadian Sustainable Development Areas Study)

8. An Example of the Atlantic Coastal Action Programme (Jim Ellsworth and Allison Lowe, Atlantic Coastal Action Programme)

9. A Comparison of the Spanish, Chinese and American Experience (Miel Corbett, author of "An Evaluation of the Effectiveness of the Coverage and Management of Biosphere reserves").

9.6 The Role of Universities in Protected Areas Management

Organizer: Neil Munro, Parks Canada

Chair: Gordon Nelson, University of Waterloo

Rapporteur: Karen Beazley, Dalhousie University

Summary

Universities and more particularly individual faculty members have had a close involvement with the evolution of policy, planning, and public consultation and in the identification, establishment and management of protected areas in Canada. They have also been instrumental in undertaking both physical and biological research as well as research in the social sciences. During this workshop, a continuation of the two other sessions on Canadian protected areas, nine presenters have given an overview and specific illustrations of this involvement, including present studies that are reflective of a more holistic or ecological approach and that are concerned with overall environment and economic issues and impacts.

Objective

To provide the participants with a general overview, and selected examples, of the significant contribution of Canadian universities to protected areas management in Canada.

Conclusions

Universities play a number of significant roles in protected area management. The primary roles relate to:

❑ provision of objective, independent, arms-length, "pure" and applied research ;

❑ training and education of students, park staff, and the public;

❑ review, reporting, observation, and assessment with regard to policy, process, planning, and management;

❑ facilitation of coordination and cooperative initiatives (round tables, task forces, workshops, committees); and

❑ broad-based communication functions (conferences, public education), especially regarding larger societal choices and values pertaining to protected areas, as well as for changing ideas in park management and planning (ecological integrity, ecosystem management, business approach, interpretative-education programmes).

Park agencies and personnel have to be aware of what is available from universities, and of the value of this actual/potential contribution.

Parks are an excellent forum in which to conduct research, because they can be used as benchmarks, and require a vast array of research initiatives.

With the above in mind, certain needs must be recognized:

❑   for a greater focus on social/behavioural/attitudinal research (versus the traditional focus on natural sciences);

❑   for a greater involvement of the public in protected area research and actions;

❑   for balancing scientific and social information (science) with public input and participation;

❑   for addressing broader landscape contexts and, in general, the role of parks in land matrix.

More cooperation and communication are needed:

❑   among universities;

❑   between universities and colleges;

❑   among universities, parks and the public as partners (social earning);

❑   among protected area partners and traditionally non-supportive groups;

❑   among those who cherish different, and at times perceived as opposite, values in protected areas;

❑   among planners, managers and researchers; and

❑   among protected area agencies and people internationally.

Cross cutting issues

In addition to the needs outlined above for enhanced cooperation and communications, public awareness and education needs to be enhanced, in spite of funding cutbacks and through more public and civic forums. In particular, the ecological function of parks needs to be highlighted, in order to balance the perception of parks as mainly recreational and touristic in nature and goals. Research, management, and education efforts need to be coordinated, prioritized, and integrated in a context of rapidly-changing societal expectations, environmental conditions, and business climate.

Outputs and Follow-up

Because this workshop had a demonstration purpose, presentations and discussions have led to conclusions only, as outlined above. There have been no formal recommendations or commitments to a formal output.

Papers and Presentations

1.   The Role of University in National Parks Research (David Gauthier, University of Regina)

2. Ecosystem Management in National Parks: Experience from Quebec (Louis Belanger, Laval University)

3. The Greater Fundy National Park Ecosystem and Model Forest (Bill Freedman, Dalhousie University)

4. The Bow Valley Study in Retrospect (Robert Page, University of Calgary)

5. Combining Science and Public Consultation in Establishing a Network of Protected Areas: An Alberta Example (Guy Swinnerton, University of Alberta)

6. National Parks and Protected Areas: A Human Ecological Decision Making (Gordon Nelson, University of Waterloo)

7. Training for Protected Areas Managers (John Marsh, Trent University).

10.1 Latin American Biodiversity Forum

Organizer: Rosario Ortiz Quijano, General Coordinator of the Latin American
Biodiversity Forum/Fundación Pro-Sierra Nevada de Santa Marta

Chair: Juan Mayr Maldonado, Fundación Pro-Sierra Nevada de Santa
Marta

Rapporteur: María José Durán, Fundación Pro-Sierra Nevada de Santa Marta

Summary

*The results of the Latin American Biodiversity Forum were presented as the product of the
work of 116 participants from 19 countries representing governments, non-governmental
organizations and both local and indigenous communities. A review of the state of the art of
legal and political aspects related to the implementation of Article 15 of the Convention on
Biological Diversity (on access to genetic resources) were presented by representatives of five
countries in the region. A presentation was made by Colombia's High Commission of Peace
about the relationship between illegal crops and loss of tropical forest.*

Objectives

1. To present the Latin American Biodiversity Forum results.

2. To enhance regional coordination and partnerships among IUCN members in the
   region related to the implementation of the Convention on Biological Diversity.

3. To contribute to the discussion and analysis of some of the underlying causes of forest and biodiversity loss from the perspective of Latin American countries.

Conclusions

Institutionalization of the Latin American Biodiversity Forum. Institutionalization of the Latin
American Biodiversity Forum will create a permanent space of discussion that will allow for
constructive debate of the main conflicts and environmental problems of the region, and in that way
give an articulated contribution to the global debate. This permanent Forum will guarantee that the
recommendations on the different subjects treated will be mobilized in a successful way. In addition,
it will facilitate greater cooperation between Latin American countries in implementing the
Convention on Biological Diversity.

Definition of a regional agenda. To define its own regional agenda is a priority in Latin American
due to the unique situation of these countries.

Traditional knowledge protection. The traditional knowledge articles of the Convention on

Biological Diversity (notably 8j and 10c) could either be accepted or rejected by these communities, depending on whether or not it will affect their traditional cultural system. This calls attention to the dangerous possibility that their knowledge will become a commodity and thus will affect the social bonds within their communities.

Underlying causes of deforestation and biodiversity loss. The workshop emphatically emphasized the necessity of including in the deforestation and biodiversity loss analysis of the underlying causes that produce these phenomena, including among other things, illegal crops, violence, consumption patterns, low standards of living, macroeconomic policies, land concentration, and cattle raising.

Outputs and Follow-up

❑ Distribution of the executive summary of the Latin American results to key actors.

❑ Exchange of experiences and development of cooperation between countries in the region on some of the Convention articles.

❑ Raise awareness of the complex and urgently needed attention to address the underlying causes of forest or biodiversity loss.

Papers and Presentations

1. Introduction (Juan Mayr Maldonado, Colombia)

2. Latin American Biodiversity Forum Results Presentation (Rosario Ortiz Quijano, Colombia)

3. Implementation of the Convention on Biological Diversity in the Latin American Region: Legal/Political Aspects, Opportunities and Obstacles

   Ecuadorian process (Luis Suarez)
   Brazilian process (Sonia Wiedmann)
   Panamanian process (Angel Urena)
   Andean process (Jorge Cailloux)
   Cuban process (Orlando Rey)

4. Illegal Crops and Loss of Tropical Forests (Alfredo Molano, Colombia).

10.2 Factoring the Environment into Corporate Planning: The Energy Sector

Organizer: David Morgan, Policy Analyst, National Round Table on the Environment and the Economy (NRTEE), Canada

Chair: Pierre Marc Johnson, former Premier of Québec and former NRTEE Vice-Chair

Rapporteur: Mitchell Beer, InfoLink Consultants Inc., Ottawa, Canada

Summary

Climate change has emerged as a key challenge for Canada's energy sector. While there is little disagreement over the need for dramatic reductions in the industry's production of greenhouse gases, implementation remains a subject of debate. Best practices within the energy sector are a useful reference point for further action. Meanwhile, discussion continues on such issues as the role of regulation, the costs and benefits of carbon taxes, and the potential impact of an international system of tradeable emission credits.

Objectives

1. To foster discussion on the role of the private sector in sustainable development, most specifically in addressing the challenge of climate change.

2. To review tangible steps that Canadian corporations have taken to incorporate sustainable development principles in their day-to-day operations.

3. To identify barriers to sustainable development within the private sector, at the levels of policy and practice.

Conclusions

Sustainable practices can benefit the bottom line. Companies that adopt sustainable development practices end up investing in technologies that also enhance productivity and profitability. The global market for environmental technologies is expected to reach C$500 billion by the end of the century, making sustainable business practice a win-win for both the environment and the economy. A corporate commitment to the environment also carries the intangible benefit of building a sense of shared commitment that brings individuals, organizations and the broader community together in pursuit of common goals.

Voluntary measures may be only one part of a global response to climate change. Canada's progress in reducing greenhouse gas emissions has been tangible, but more gradual than many might like. An international system of tradeable emission credits would open the door for Canadian-based energy companies to invest scarce remediation dollars where they will have the greatest impact. While carbon taxes are described as "punitive" by energy industry representatives, environmentalists consider that change within the industry has been too slow and superficial. Rapid reductions in greenhouse gas emissions may be held up by "climate change denial", combined with the 15- to 50-year time span that is required to replace existing infrastructure. A transition to a lower-carbon economy would include more balanced tax treatment of energy efficiency and renewable energy technologies in relation to conventional supply sources, as well as a broader corporate commitment (from auto manufacturers, for example) to stop designing and promoting consumer products that contribute to the climate change crisis.

Deregulation of the power sector represents a major challenge for sustainable development. Competitive trends, particularly in the North American electricity industry, have drawn attention and resources away from environmental affairs and technology research. Electricity deregulation will bring new economic imperatives in support of energy efficiency and demand-side management – while consumer prices will remain low, power utilities will face pressure to postpone construction of new capacity. There will also be less interest in renewable electricity generated by independent power producers. If governments do not learn to distinguish between "command and control" regulatory systems and performance-based regulation, North American environmental standards could be gutted.

Outputs and Follow-up

❑ A detailed conference report was produced in the week following the workshop.

❑ Workshop content has been incorporated into the Round Table's preparations for the upcoming Rio+5 conference, and in its ongoing work with partners in the Pacific Rim.

❑ A recent Plenary Session of the National Round Table dealt primarily with Canada's response to climate change, including the role of the energy sector.

Papers and Presentations

1. Business Strategies for Sustainable Development in the Canadian Energy Sector (Ralph Torrie of Torrie Smith Associates)

Spoken remarks from the following:

2. Hon. Sergio Marchi, Minister of the Environment, Canada

3. Pierre Marc Johnson, former Premier of Québec and former vice-chair, National Round Table on the Environment and the Economy

4. James Leslie, Senior Vice-President of Sustainable Development, TransAlta Corp.

5. Denise Therrien, Vice-President, Environment and Community Affairs, Hydro-Québec

6. Alain Perez, President, Canadian Petroleum Products Institute

7. André Delisle, President, Transfert Environnement

8. Rob Macintosh, Policy Director, Pembina Institute for Appropriate Development

9. Susan Holtz, environment consultant and former NRTEE vice-chair.

10.3 Indigenous People's Knowledge and Practice in Natural Resource Management

Organizer: Eduardo Fernandez, IUCN-US

Chair: Gonzalo Oviedo

Rapporteur: Donna Leaman

Summary

Indigenous peoples are important actors in environmental conservation, but too often they are excluded from conservation activities by governments and major conservation organizations. Indigenous Peoples organizations are open to developing an alliance with the conservation movement. This workshop was an opportunity to strengthen links and develop a joint discussion on how to achieve conservation. Open institutional spaces for indigenous peoples participation in policy development is a precondition to cooperate.

Objectives

1. To facilitate the development of global policies on indigenous knowledge and practice on natural resource management, through the facilitation of a discussion among the different IUCN Indigenous Peoples and Conservation Initiative (IPCI) networks, working groups and task forces.

2. To present and discuss the work of the Regional Networks, Task Forces and Working Groups on Indigenous Peoples within the IPCI.

3. To review the status of implementation of General Assembly Resolutions 19.20, 19.21, 19.22 and 19.67, and others relevant to indigenous peoples.

4. To develop global policy recommendations from the lessons gathered from the regional networks.

5. To advocate and create awareness amongst other workshops, for incorporation of indigenous knowledge and practices in the development of policies and design of projects for the region.

6. To develop and propose recommendations and resolutions concerning indigenous peoples, conservation, resource use and management for adoption by the World Conservation Congress.

7. To discuss the follow up to the IPCI.

Conclusions

Indigenous peoples need to be consulted. Indigenous peoples are the real actors in conservation, but do not get recognition for this from governments or conservation NGOs.

Support for UN Declaration on the Rights of Indigenous Peoples. There is support for the UN Draft Declaration on the Rights of Indigenous Peoples and for the process of consultation with indigenous peoples, and a call for IUCN to support ratification of the Declaration by its members.

IUCN should provide institutional and financial support to indigenous peoples. IUCN is called upon to fulfil its commitment to indigenous peoples through institutional and financial support, and improved integration of indigenous peoples interests in the work of programmes and commissions.

Cross-cutting issues

In the area of communications, IUCN must use its networks and members to better communicate the concerns of indigenous peoples with respect to sustainable resource management and use. In terms of law, IUCN is called upon to support the Draft Declaration on the Rights of Indigenous Peoples.

Outputs and Follow-up

1. The book *Indigenous Peoples and Sustainability* was published and distributed.
2. Agreements with Indigenous Peoples' organizations are in process.
3. Six resolutions dealing with concerns of indigenous peoples were adopted by the WCC.

Papers and Presentations

1. Opening of Welcome (Eduardo Fernandez. Coordinator, IP&C Initiative, IUCN)
2. Indigenous Peoples Territories, Biodiversity, and Tourism: The Experience of Kuna Yala (Eligio Alvarado, Presidente Asociacion Dobbo Yala, Panama)
3. Emerging New Legal Standards for Comprehensive Rights for Indigenous Peoples: Future Directions for Environmental Lawyers (Johanna Sutherland, IUCN Commission on Environmental Law)
4. Indigenous Peoples, Biodiversity, and Intellectual Property Rights: The Southern Africa Experience (Andrew Mushita, COMMUTECH, Zimbabwe)
5. Indigenous Peoples and Biodiversity: Conservation in the Arctic (Finn Lyne, Inuit)
6. Indigenous Peoples of the North America Conservation Strategy (Jacky Waledo, International Indian Treaty Council)
7. Indigenous Knowledge Systems: The Southern Africa Experience (Nakatiwa Mulkita, ZERO, Zimbabwe)
8. Pueblos Indigenas y Manejo de Recursos Naturales (Letter from Valerio Grefa. Coordinator of COICA, Coordinadora de las Organizaciones Indigenas de la Cuenca Amazonica)
9. Discussion with Councillors Alicia Barcena and Alejandra Sanchez on the process for modification and adoption of the resolutions presented by indigenous peoples delegates.

10.4 Landscape Conservation

Organizer: Bryn Green, CESP Landscape Conservation Working Group

Chair: Ted Trzyna, California Institute of Public Affairs

Rapporteur: Catherine Bickmore, CB Associates

Summary

The ecological and socio-economic vulnerability of isolated protected areas has in the past decade led to a realization that conservation objectives can only be realized on a large template – the landscape. Recent advances in landscape ecology and planning have great potential to serve as mechanisms to facilitate more effective conservation.

Objectives

1. To report on the CESP-LCWG activities in implementing Resolution 19/40 of the Buenos Aires General Assembly, namely to undertake a pilot study to identify threatened landscapes and bring together researchers and practitioners to prepare case studies for holistic landscape conservation.

2. To consider some of the main threats to landscapes and review some of the methodological approaches made to address them.

3. To relate the work of the CESP-LCWG to cognate approaches elsewhere in other IUCN commissions, and explore the most effective ways of promoting landscape conservation within IUCN.

Conclusions

Landscape description and assessment. The concept of landscape gives expression to the products of the spatial and temporal interaction of people with the environment. A landscape may be conceived as a particular configuration of topography, vegetation cover, land-use and settlement pattern which delimits some coherence of natural, historical and cultural processes and activities. Landscapes set protected areas into more ecologically and culturally viable contexts and are increasingly employed as the basis for strategic planning and management.

A questionnaire survey of landscape professionals made by the CESP-LCWG in collaboration with the WCMC solicited some 30 descriptions of threatened landscapes in a pilot study to test procedures for their identification. Most were from Europe where the membership of the LCWG is mainly concentrated, but considerable interest was also revealed in Japan, China and Australia. They covered a wide range of landscape types and, in Europe, can be placed into emerging landscape classifications.

Landscape dynamics: natural and human disturbance. The biodiversity and cherished features of many landscapes are the direct result of human intervention, which often mimics natural disturbance.

While traditional exploitation incidentally maintained them, many landscapes are now precariously balanced between extensification/abandonment and intensification. Modern agriculture, forestry, water management and tourism were identified as the major threats to most landscapes in the pilot study.

The objectives of maintaining cultural landscapes are often unclear and the costs very high. It is unrealistic and socially unacceptable to retain fossilized landscapes. The marginal ways of life which maintain many cultural landscapes are hard and socio-economic systems cannot be prevented from evolving into more comfortable life styles. New 21st century landscapes may be able to be designed and established which incorporate past and present cultural features while exploiting resources more sustainably.

Integrating principles and practice: translating research into policy. The CESP-LCWG consists of both academics and landscape planners and managers. Progress has been made in making the results of research available in a form useful to practitioners through landscape case studies, or "green books". The first has been published for the landscapes of Western Crete. Future development might possibly relate such handbooks to landscape types rather than individual landscapes.

Outputs and Follow-up

❑ Publication of the draft report of the CESP-LCWG made available in Montreal.

❑ Developing the pilot-study into a full-scale survey of threatened landscapes to be undertaken by the WCMC.

❑ Extending the activities of the LCWG, begun in Europe, to other parts of the world.

❑ Discussions between CESP, CNPPA and CEM on future directions of landscape work in IUCN.

❑ Collaboration was established with major European landscape initiatives to document European landscapes (EU and European Environment Agency) and to establish a European Landscape Convention (Council of Europe). Links were also developed with UNESCO to ensure that national and regional landscape initiatives nest with the global action under the World Heritage Convention.

Papers and Presentations

1. Introduction: People and Place (Ted Trzyna, California Institute of Public Affairs)

2. Red Listing for Protecting Threatened, Valued Landscapes (Yoav Sagi, Israel Society for the Protection of Nature)

3. Territorial Systems Of Ecological Stability: A New Legal Conception in Slovakia (Ladislav Miklos, Slovak Academy of Sciences)

4. Mass Tourism and the Heterogeneity of Coastal Balearic Landscapes (Miguel Morey, University of Balearic Islands)

5. Landscape Ecology into Land Use: Research into Practice (Bryn Green, University of London)

6. Conclusions: Shaping Sustainable Landscapes (Catherine Bickmore, CB Associates, London).

10.5 Sustainable Development: Lessons from the South

Organizer: Sustainable Development Policy Institute

Chair: Mohammad al-Sahnoun

Rapporteur: Mehreen Samee

Summary

Conservation issues in the South are different from those in the North, and therefore require different approaches. Because rural populations in developing countries often directly depend on their local natural resource base, a participatory multi-stakeholder process is needed if conservation efforts are to be "owned" by a large cross-section of society. Furthermore, issues of equity and appropriate technology for a sustainable livelihood need to be moved to the forefront of the conservation agenda.

Objectives

1. To highlight the unique nature of sustainable development problems faced by southern countries, as being distinct from those of the North.

2. To emphasize that creative solutions to these problems have to be different from those applied in northern countries.

3. To underscore the undesirability of transferring solutions developed in the North to the South.

4. To understand how global decisions affect national and local policies and impact the lives of people at the micro level.

Conclusions

Experiences of the South vis-à-vis responses to policy, influencing policy, interaction between humans and the environment, and institutional development are unique. The prevalent approach that environmental problems in the South can best be tackled by transferring solutions developed in the North is inappropriate, since conservation problems faced by the South are distinct from those of the North. In the South a large number of people (mostly marginalized) depend for livelihoods on the natural resource base. Any conservation strategy which does not take into account the cultural context or the effect of conservation efforts on the livelihoods of the local population is bound to fail.

Due emphasis needs to be placed on the process which leads to conservation, which may be more important than the product or outcome of strategies and projects aimed at sustainable development. A participatory multi-stakeholder process is needed if the strategy/project is to be owned by a large cross-section of society. A wide-based ownership – including local communities, civil society, mass media, acadaemia and the research community, private sector, and decision-makers – will ensure greater chances of success for the project/strategy.

Technological innovation for sustainable development in southern countries has to be not only appropriate but also appropriable – not simply low-cost but also such that it can be absorbed given the institutional structures prevalent in society.

The objective of all global environmental and economic agreements should be protecting the rights of the weak and marginalized (both at national and local levels). Unless the global agenda is equitable, the objective of realizing a sustainable world will not be realized. Technological innovations should ensure a sustained livelihood for the marginalized without destroying the resource base. Involvement of local enterprises in both production and marketing of the technology is a pre-requisite for sustainability.

Outputs and Follow-up

❑   The Union must shift its narrow focus on conservation of the natural environment to making conservation people-centred.

❑   Participatory approaches to conservation should be encouraged. In this sense the use of collaborative management as a tool may be useful.

❑   Any strategy for conservation should be developed in collaboration with multiple stakeholders.

Papers and Presentations

1.   Workshop Objectives (Tariq Banuri, Sustainable Development Policy Institute, Pakistan)

2.   How to Influence Policy: The Pakistan NCS Story (Aban Marker Kabraji, IUCN Pakistan/David Runnals, International Development Research Centre, Canada)

3.   Collaborative Management for Sustainable Development (Richard Sandbrook, International Institute for Environment and Development, UK)

4.   Technology for Sustainable Development (Ashok Khosla, Development Alternatives, India)

5.   Governance for Sustainable Development (Augusta Henriques, Tiniguena, Guinea-Bissau)

6.   The Global Agenda for the South (Atiq Rahman, Bangladesh Centre for Advanced Studies, Bangladesh).

Reports from the
Cross-Cutting Themes

Report on Cross-Cutting Issues in Workshops: Gender

Rapporteur: Miriam Wyman

Background

The need for IUCN to consider gender issues has arisen regularly since the 1984 General Assembly. Resolutions have been passed on the issue, consultants have written reports stressing its importance, and the first Christoffersen Report highlighted the need to integrate gender issues fully into all IUCN programmes rather than treating them as a separate activity. In the April 1996 meeting of the Policy Committee, Council recommended that one way to ensure that gender issues become integrated into IUCN's policy and programmes would be to deliberately incorporate them into all workshops at the Montreal Congress.

"Gender" refers to the social and cultural functions of men and women. For IUCN, using gender analysis means looking at how the differing functions and roles of men and women relate to sustainable development and conservation efforts and vice-versa. It means that policy makers and project planners within the IUCN constituency should consider the different impacts on and potential contributions of women and men in this context. It is now becoming accepted that ignoring the importance of gender-determined roles may have consequences detrimental to both the men and women of the society affected and to the conservation effort itself.

To help this process of integrating gender perspectives into the Congress workshops, three key gender questions were developed by staff and Councillors:

1. Was gender analysis done in the case/situation presented? If so, what impact on conservation has the inclusion of the gender analysis had? If not, how could a greater knowledge of gender roles help/have helped in this initiative?

2. Have women been involved in all stages of the initiative, both in the defining of policies and in their implementation? If so, how? If not, what steps have been considered to remedy this?

3. How has the initiative affected traditional division of labour, access and control of resources and distribution of benefits between the sexes? What have been the positive and negative impacts on women?

These questions were distributed to Workshop Stream Coordinators who were expected to relay them to Workshop Chairs, presenters and panellists and rapporteurs and were distributed again early in the Congress.

The Monitoring Exercise

The approach taken to assess the extent to which the key gender questions were integrated into presentations and discussions was multifaceted.

A team of volunteers was recruited from among IUCN staff, Councillors and membership in advance of and during the Congress to participate in monitoring the Congress workshops for gender discussion and contributing to it where appropriate. By the end of the Congress, more than thirty women and men were part of the Team, led by a consultant engaged for the purpose, and a number of others followed the work though they were unable to participate in daily meetings. Backgrounds, ages, cultures and experiences ranged widely, which made for insightful and reflective comment and discussion.

The Team held a preliminary meeting to review plans to monitor each workshop and discuss with the Chief Rapporteur his needs for the report to the Final Plenary. The team agreed to meet each morning during the Congress to ensure that workshops and non-workshop events were covered, to review experiences of the previous day and to share general observations.

Information about the Gender Resource Team was posted around the Congress building and in the *Ookpik*, the daily Congress newsletter. The gender initiative was also introduced at IUCN staff meetings and individual conversations related to the gender initiative were undertaken with a range of IUCN staff members and Councillors – people who were interested and supportive of the initiative but whose additional Congress obligations prevented them from participating actively

To assist the team in documenting the extent to which the key gender questions were integrated into the presentations and discussions and to note any additional observations and advice for the future, an evaluation form was developed and circulated to team members and workshop organizers.

In accordance with plans to assist the Chief Rapporteur with his report to plenary, a two page report was prepared based on a preliminary analysis of those forms submitted up to the evening of October 19 (a total of eighty-two forms were submitted and integrated into the group's final report). The Report to the Final Plenary addressed several gender issues, including equity and the need to include consideration of gender roles in conservation activities, but did not mention explicitly the gender initiative. Two panellists during the Final Plenary also referred to gender issues and the importance of gender with respect to sustainable development as well as conservation.

Once the workshops were over, the Gender Resource Team held an assessment session to:

❏ review the experience in the workshops with respect to the gender questions and the extent to which gender perspectives were reflected;

❏ discuss how to improve future Congresses;

❏ discuss how to move forward on gender issues within IUCN.

Outcome

The gender initiative follows many years of study and consideration, and was an important effort to "implement" gender. It provided clear information about the status of gender considerations at the Congress and, by extension, the kind of attention given to gender in IUCN's work. In this sense, gender at the Congress is only part of a set of larger issues regarding gender for IUCN as a whole.

Key Gender Questions were not integrated into Congress Workshops. The key gender questions were not included in any significant way in the Congress workshops. Since the key gender questions were sent to Workshop Stream Coordinators well before the Congress, it was expected that gender would be included in presentations or, if not, that this "gap" would be acknowledged, and that Chairs of each session might raise questions about the extent to which the key gender questions were considered.

In only a few cases, however, were gender questions raised by the Workshop Chair or a Presenter and, in most cases, treatment was superficial. More often, questions about gender analysis came from the floor and were noted but rarely addressed. The tone in which questions were addressed ranged from supportive and encouraging, to apologetic, to dismissive and adversarial. In a number of cases, questions were acknowledged but not answered.

Numbers are telling. Men presenters and panellists far outnumbered women. Overall, one in four presenters was a woman. In some cases, there were as many as fifteen male presenters and no women. These numbers suggest that little attention was given to gender balance in Congress sessions. Numbers alone are a rather superficial reflection of the situation with respect to gender; nonetheless, the Gender Resource Team felt that this situation reflects IUCN as a whole.

Overall, gender analysis was absent. The large majority of initiatives presented at the Congress did not incorporate gender perspectives. In only a few cases was information presented which disaggregated data and looked separately at participation of women and men as well as impacts on women and men. It became very apparent that one of the reasons for the absence of gender analysis was the lack of understanding regarding what gender analysis is, how to do it, and what its benefits can be.

The key gender questions did, however, seem to have some effect in raising awareness of gender issues. Some workshops gave passing reference to the idea and acknowledgement that gender analysis is important. Also, although gender discussion was not a prominent part of the workshops, discussion about gender was taking place in informal conversations throughout the Congress. Nonetheless, gender rhetoric is no substitute for gender analysis.

Congress structure often made it difficult to raise gender questions. Many workshops had multiple presenters, each of whom gave general overviews. This meant there was little time for discussion of concepts, processes or methodologies. Workshops often operated at a very high level of generality which made it difficult for participants to debate and come to grips with the many complex challenges in our work. It was difficult to put a "human face" on the many situations under discussion.

Gender Resolution provides a mandate. An important resolution on gender was brought forward by the Central American members and was accepted by the IUCN membership with virtually no opposition. The resolution provides a mandate for IUCN to formulate a gender programme and policy, to promote participation and representation of women within IUCN, to integrate gender perspectives across IUCN's programme, to provide technical and financial support for gender initiatives, and to establish a Working Group on Gender and Sustainable Development to ensure that the resolution is followed and incorporated into the IUCN programme. Its acceptance demonstrates the recognition, in principle, of the importance of gender, and it lays the groundwork for development of a clear action plan with respect to integrating gender.

The Gender Resource Team was itself a significant Congress event. The nature of the group and the range of backgrounds and experience allowed for a broad range of observations and stimulated reflection, serious questions, and thoughtful discussion among Team members. There was unanimous agreement that the Gender Resource Team served an important function, and should be continued – at future Congresses and possibly in the ongoing work of integrating gender into IUCN's work.

Commitment and support already exist. Over a number of years, IUCN has investigated gender policies and ways to integrate gender considerations into all aspects of its work. There is considerable support for taking significant steps forward – at Headquarters, among regional staff, among Councillors, and throughout the membership. There is also some excellent experience with this issue and great willingness to share it.

Suggestions for Future Congresses

The single most significant recommendation coming out of the gender initiative was to ensure that **gender issues are an inherent element of the Congress system**, from initial planning to briefings at the Congress itself. Those planning the Congress must:

❑ Integrate specific expectations regarding gender (such as references to levels of participation and how roles affect implementation of projects) into all information for future Congresses and ensure that it reaches everyone involved – this would serve to raise expectations and to encourage raising of relevant questions.

❑ Invite very specific input – for example, practical programmes, success stories, etc.

❑ Ensure a more equal balance between men and women Chairs, Moderators, Presenters and Panellists; be consistently aware of the need for gender balance. This would be made easier with the assembly of a database of qualified women who might fill these positions.

❑ Organize at least one high-level panel on gender issues as related to conservation – why it is important, where programmes have gone wrong because differential involvement and impacts were not taken into account, where there are successes as a result of careful gender analysis.

❑ Have key people provide clear support and expectations for integrating gender. For example, presentations on gender by the head of each national or regional office would demonstrate that gender was being taken seriously.

❑ Hold advance briefings for Workshop Chairs to assist them in posing relevant questions, encouraging participation, recognizing moments when gender-related topics arise, and ensuring that the tone taken with respect to gender issues not be dismissive, frivolous or antagonistic.

❑ Convene a Gender Resource Team to support efforts to integrate gender and conservation. The success of the Gender Resource Team in monitoring the gender initiative and in raising awareness of gender at the Congress suggests that this model should be repeated at future Congresses.

❑ Continue to regard gender as a cross-cutting issue and not one that is confined to specific sessions.

Report on Cross-Cutting Issues in Workshops: Communication

Rapporteur: Wendy Goldstein

Introduction

Becoming more conscious of what it means to communicate with people outside of the environment circle is an imperative for success of IUCN's mission. How well are the Union's members and Commissions dealing with communication in a structured and strategic way?

Before the Congress, all workshop organisers were asked to consider drawing attention to the role of communication by presenters in their sessions, just as they were asked to consider gender issues.

Aside from the workshops, the issue of communication had a reasonable profile during the Congress. During plenary sessions the Director General expressed concern on repeated occasions that, "The Union has at no stage of its evolution paid sufficient attention to communications – to getting its messages out to those who need to hear them"..... "so far we (IUCN) have been inadequate and we are not fulfilling our mandate. I don't find IUCN reports of hundreds of pages useful in helping the key learning from our projects to be shared."

IUCN Corporate Communication

This message was reiterated at a special meeting of experts from the Commission on Education and Communication as well as from member organisations. The purpose was to discuss corporate communication, seek a mandate from the members to lead a communication strategy for the Union and to reflect on the first steps IUCN had taken. The Director General concluded, "our members need to have IUCN known to help them with their own work and to be better able to use our policy and technical influence. Effective communication is also vital for our funding support and we need professional help."

Ammirati Puris Lintas, an advertising agency, had prepared the building blocks of a communication strategy designed to move people from being tacit supporters to active subscribers. IUCN has to define who it is and what it stands for, and needs to be able to say the right thing at the right time. IUCN has both internal (within IUCN, between members) and external (to outside world) communication needs. Internal communication would build a sense of coherence, team work and more efficient use of resources. This internal culture will determine the external face of the organization; internal communication is the glue to make an organisation strong.

For members, corporate communication increases the value of the organisation to them, makes the organisation better known , shares information, and increases networking and complimentarity. The external communication provides a better understanding of IUCN's mission, profile, and identity, which in turn will open doors.

IUCN's diversity is a strength but also creates communication problems. The presentation showed how other complex organisations can communicate its core business. It also showed an idea for how an appeal to emotion can be used in communicating about IUCN's work.

Participants agreed that IUCN certainly is little known. IUCN's personality needs defining as does its positioning and who and why people have to know about us. A detailed briefing is required before the real skills of the agency can be brought to bear on the organisation's communication. IUCN should concentrate on corporate communication, use top down and bottom up processes to reflect decentralisation, take it step by step and don't discard the logo since a lot of work was done on that already.

Workshops and Environmental Communication

Members of the Commission on Education and Communication attended all workshop streams to monitor the attention to communication in the work reported. Questions were designed to ask speakers, as a way to draw out how they managed to engage people. It was very difficult in many streams to have time to ask a question and sometimes there was no context for the question.

Attention to the role of communication was not made clear in many presentations. Others presented efforts at creating awareness. Some mentioned participation, but what does it mean to handle these processes? Did it lead to the desired improvement for the environment? We didn't find out. Are conservationists really clear about exactly what changes need to happen? Were those ideas for change explicit, valid, and did they happen?

The marine workshop had some examples of resources made for educational purposes, and the international network was able to benefit by exchange of these materials. By all accounts the collaborative management discussions were very much about communication and empowerment.

CEC members made a number of observations on the conduct of workshops at the next WCC. Some workshops had a very "in crowd" feel to them, making new members to the group uncomfortable; not the best when the public are invited. Others were terribly boring, being a stream of presentations, with no questions and no feedback. What about communicating effectively? Dialogue? Moreover some presenters had scratchily prepared overhead sheets with pages of script writing – is this good enough? We need guidelines on making presentations for the next WCC.

Perhaps we should change the name from "workshops" to "panels" or "paper sessions". If we do want workshops, then we need more participatory processes that build together ideas, concepts and strategies using techniques like Visualisation in Participatory Processes. It was even suggested that the Commission on Education and Communication should manage the overall workshop round to develop better cross-sectoral discussions and assist the workshop process to come up with results.

The stream on Strategies for Sustainability demonstrated how communication is a key to implementing a strategy. Experience from the field showed that communication must be an integrated part of all conservation initiatives because it is communication that so often makes the difference between success and failure. Even though some effort to provide an interactive experience in communication planning was used, next time CEC would like to manage a more participatory process. It is a definite challenge in the multi-lingual context of the Congress.

At the WCC in Montreal, programme managers and practitioners called for increased support in the area of communication. They expressed the need for training and professional development to assist them in influencing policy and decision-making at all levels and with all target groups responsible for environmental problems. They said they needed more guidance on participatory communication methods, planning and conceptualising communication, managing communication and effective research, monitoring and evaluation. They spoke of the need to translate communication strategies into realistic action plans designed to bring about lasting change among various target groups. They said that much of the effort to date has concentrated on creating awareness, and that the more difficult work of behaviour change lay ahead.

Many expressed frustration in dealing with donors who, without a common conceptual framework for communication and mechanisms to co-ordinate their activities, place conflicting demands on field managers and hold vastly different expectations for them. In frustration, many field managers take the path of least resistance, devoting the bulk of their communication efforts to public relations and materials. Some field staff also called for clearer direction and leadership from IUCN with regard to communication.

Communicators and program managers valued the learning experience in the WCC workshops on communication and called for similar support to be made available at country and operational levels. They voiced the need for practical tools, guidance and support from development communication professionals, linkages with other practitioners and resources, and opportunities to learn from successful field projects.

Communication experts at the Congress emphasised that behavioural change is a complex, difficult process, often requiring 7-10 years of sustained effort in order to produce results. Field staff called on IUCN and its members to double their efforts to support them toward this end.

With regard to the successful implementation of conservation strategies, the major communication issues and challenges appear to be the following:

❑ wide gap between awareness and action;

❑ lack of skills among field managers to analyse, plan, integrate and manage communication that leads to change;

❑ inadequate or inappropriate use of communication (e.g., flawed national communication planning, lack of rigorous situation analyses and the substitution of products, such as pamphlets posters and radio and television spots, for interactive communication *processes* directed at behavioural change);

❑ confusion at policy and decision-making levels about the role of communication (e.g., imprecise use of the terms "education" and "communication");

❑ insufficient human and financial resources to sustain effective communication programming;

❑ lack of political will for action on the part of some country partners;

❑ lack of donor coordination; and

❑ lack of case materials from the environment sector.

The Way Forward

Little progress can be made in bridging the gap between awareness and action without a cadre of communication specialists at regional and national levels within the environmental sector, as there is in other sectors in some countries. A priority of IUCN and its partners should be to create this cadre through training and professional development. But to achieve this objective requires much more than conventional workshops and seminars. (Many who attended the WCC had been exposed to communication training, yet felt ill-equipped to meet the challenges in the field.)

Training and professional development needs to be relevant and of high quality with respect to resource persons and methodologies. To be effective, training needs to be sustained over a period of time and followed up with refresher courses and good supervision.

Communication also has to have institutional support, requiring decision makers to understand its role, ensure its integration into all relevant activities and provide resources for strategic communication to happen. Project and programme managers must support and provide leadership to staff involved in communication activities. To carry out this responsibility, they require an understanding of environment /development communication and its application in the field of conservation.

More work is needed in documenting, disseminating and applying the lessons learned from communication field work.

Greater effort is required to link those responsible for communication with people, networks, organisations and material resources. The synergy that comes with organisational alliances and the mobilisation of civil society is necessary to achieve lasting results.

Conclusions

IUCN has prompted and assisted much of the process that has yielded national and regional conservation strategies and action plans. Yet, there remains in most countries an enormous gap between awareness and action. IUCN risks losing credibility unless more is done to close this gap. Communication – one of the most potent means to affect change – must remain a high priority of IUCN.

These conclusions are based on the several communication workshops in the Congress and discussions with Congress delegates. They are intended to capture some of the strongly articulated needs of people working at community and field levels and the major communication issues and challenges facing IUCN, its members and other key stakeholders in their efforts to bring about change.

IUCN should take the lead in training and professional development at the national and sub-national level, building capacity, fostering a better understanding of communication and improving the management of communication from the bottom up and the top down. Strengthening the capacity for communication analysis and planning must be a priority. A quick response to the Montreal experience is essential, hence the first recommendation.

Recommended Action over the Short Term

IUCN should establish a training/professional development programme in three countries on an experimental basis. It should closely monitor and evaluate the programme and apply the lessons learned on a wider scale, as resources permit.

IUCN should prepare a resource book for environmental communicators. There is a growing body of literature and resource materials in the field of development communication, much of it related to health, water and sanitation and agriculture. However, relatively few resources are designed specifically for communicators and programme managers in the environment field.

While many agree on the need for resource materials, they will have little impact unless tied to a training initiative. Field workers at the WCC emphasised this point. They said that manuals and handbooks are rarely used; unless individuals have a solid background in the subject area, they are unlikely to adapt the materials to their particular development context.

Should IUCN embark on further training and professional development in communication, there is merit in producing a variety of learning materials. An outline of a resource book to supplement training was provided. It focuses on conceptualising and planning communication, two areas of great importance and greatest weakness. It would provide a number of practical tools, approaches and best practices from the field.

Should IUCN wish to proceed in producing this resource book, it should hire a consultant to draft the text and that it create a small review committee from among the communication professionals at the WCC. It would require 6–10 months to prepare a final draft.

Recommended Action over the Long-term

As a long-term strategy, IUCN should work with others to institutionalise communication training and professional development with a focus on conservation. Few institutes provide professional development and related resources and services in development communication, and none focus exclusively on conservation. While it may not be feasible to create institutes to serve the needs of the environmental sector alone, it makes sense to combine efforts with health, agriculture and other sectors that rely on communication for development.

IUCN should provide advocacy and guidance to the development cooperation community. IUCN should put environmental communication on the agenda of the development cooperation community since it is an instrument for success of environmental policy, strategies, and projects. IUCN should work with partners to present the case for environmental communication guidelines and greater investment in capacity development programmes for environmental communication.

Report on Cross-Cutting Issues in Workshops: Law

Rapporteur: Lother Gundling, IUCN Environmental Law Centre

Introduction

Law has been sometimes an obstacle, sometimes a catalyst, but is generally considered a necessary element for successful initiatives in conservation and sustainable development. Treatment of the role of law during World Conservation Congress workshops ranged from extensive debate to exclusion from the discussions. Legal issues were prominently discussed in the workshops on integrated coastal and marine management, collaborative management, and trade and the environment. Law was generally discussed in the majority of the other workshops. Discussion was actually cut off in one workshop, where the moderator ruled a law-related question as outside the scope of the debate.

Lawyers made formal presentations in 10 workshops. The frequency with which international and national legal issues were spontaneously raised in discussions during other workshops indicates increased awareness among specialists in non-legal disciplines of the role law can play in achieving conservation objectives. The discussions highlighted many issues, such as implementation of the World Heritage Convention, development of conservation strategies, and collaborative management, in which lawyers should become more involved.

International Law

The importance of international agreements in establishing global obligations for conservation and sustainable development is not disputed – the significance of CITES for wildlife conservation, and the number of States which have ratified the Convention on Biological Diversity (CBD) are evidence of this. The debates centred rather on how to make implementation of existing agreements more effective and on the form that new agreements should take. It was stressed that work on new international agreements should not be used as an excuse to delay implementation of existing ones.

Synergy and coordination among existing international agreements will be increasingly required for effective implementation of all of them. This issue was raised particularly in the context of marine law, the World Heritage Convention and the Climate Change Convention. A proposal was made to integrate implementation of the CBD and the Desertification Convention, to give national implementation strategies and plans more political weight. Another proposal called for a study exploring the links among all the major conservation conventions to draw out common measures for implementation, particularly concerning protected areas.

The trade and environment workshop clearly demonstrated that the issue is largely law-based. Modifications to relevant international legal instruments might be necessary. Particular attention must be given to the problem of defining the appropriate relationship between TRIPS and the Convention on Biological Diversity.

International law on forest conservation is fragmented. The international climate change regime might provide an example of how to develop an international regime for forests in its integration of sound scientific advice with law and policy-making. Other legal issues to be studied are how to address temperate and boreal forests as well as tropical forests, the relationship between GATT and the international forest regime, and the potential of regional instruments.

National Law

There are more laws than there are effective enforcement mechanisms. Many laws are useful, but institutional and jurisdictional conflicts impede their enforcement.

Non-existent or ineffective enforcement has emerged as a principal concern in the field of environmental law. In some cases, improving enforcement will require new legislation and institutional reform. In almost all cases in developing countries it will require capacity building.

Environmental provisions in constitutions provide important support for enforcing environmental laws. More and more countries include such provisions in their constitutions, for example on private property, on the management of natural resources, on the right to a clean environment; and on obligations of the state to protect and conserve nature and natural resources.

Litigation is another means to enhance compliance with conservation legislation. Legal rules are needed in many countries to provide citizens and environmental groups with standing to sue to enforce existing laws, or liberalize current requirements for standing.

Workshop discussions noted that national legislation in many countries is still inadequate in several areas – particularly land tenure and use, economic incentives, measures concerning sustainable use of wildlife, alien species, and implementing international agreements.

The process of developing national and local strategies must begin with the legal and institutional frameworks required to implement them, so legal issues played a prominent role in the debates about conservation strategies and collaborative management. Legal provisions facilitating collaborative management agreements must be included in general and sectoral national laws, and obstacles such as the centralized resource management frameworks existing in many countries need to be removed. Legal arrangements for collaborative management should include private law instruments such as shareholding arrangements as well as public law mechanisms, and should provide for enforcement.

The role of indigenous peoples in managing natural resources and conserving biodiversity needs to be legally recognized, through measures including constitutional and legislative provisions guaranteeing their land rights and including them in collaborative management regimes.

Environmental law reflects how societies value the environment and conservation of its components. At this stage in the development of both international and national environmental law, values need to be clarified. Two framework documents are proposed for that purpose: the Draft Covenant on Environment and Development prepared by the IUCN Commission on Environmental Law; and the Earth Charter, being developed by the Earth Council. If adopted by governments, the Covenant would be a legally-binding statement of the value they accord to conservation and sustainable development. The Earth Charter is designed to be "soft law", not legally-binding, but nevertheless a strong statement of the value human beings place on their natural environment. The two instruments would complement each other.

Reports from the
Special Events

Special Event: Communicating the Environment

Chair: Lloyd Timberlake

Panel members: David Bellamy, University of Durham and the University of Nottingham (UK); Kalpana Sharma, editor assistant of the newspaper The Hindu (India), Claude Martin, Director General of WWF-International

Rapporteur: Juanita Castano, IUCN-SUR

Introduction by the Chair

Lloyd Timberlake pointed out that the challenge for environmental organizations is that the information received by people needs to be better understood by them. Environmental issues and participation belong to the people, to everybody. Environmental groups need to lobby more successfully. Many people who work for conservation do not know how to communicate. The concept of Sustainable Management is virtually unknown, but everybody knows about issues related with human rights and the rights of women, Indian people and children. Communication about environmental issues has always been directed to the same group of people: to us.

Presentations by Panel Members

David Bellamy said that although there had been advances in the environmental movement that have allowed UNCED and this Congress to be held, environmental problems still continue: thus we still have problems with coral reefs, fisheries, pollution, eutrophication, etc. There is no agreement about new forms of energy sources. We have failed to save biodiversity which is threatened more and more each day.

Communications media play an important role in the treatment of these problems, especially at the local level. Many of the solutions are root solutions and have to be addressed with courage. The ecological movement should show more political power. Good news must also be published and the principles of Agenda 21 have to be taken into account. A well-informed youth will follow the road opened by veterans in conservation. Two major aspects of conservation need to be addressed:

❑ Sustainable management, including environmentally-sustainable tourism

❑ Sustainable scenarios where people are involved.

Through improved communications, public pressure can be mobilized to save natural treasures of global significance, such as the Galapagos Islands and Indonesia's biodiversity.

Kalpana Sharma highlighted the need to understand how the media work. Some people still have the wrong idea about them: media want to do business and they are not altruists. News agencies focus on the facts and not on the processes that drive towards or come from those facts. Only bad news or news about important people generally appear, but people who do good things are of much less news interest. The most shocking news, as for example the Bhopal tragedy in India, can develop a very big environmental consciousness. This happens because the story exceeds the environmental subject and turns to a political and economic issue.

The media have great impact on political decisions and could be important partners for conservation. Nevertheless, many limitations and needs are apparent: key persons in the communications media should be identified; journalists generally know very little about the environment because it is not a profitable specialization; and it is necessary to build environmental capacity among journalists.

Claude Martin pointed out that communications is a profession and a conservationist is not necessarily a communicator though he might have something to say. WWF has seen the need to have professionals to communicate their messages. Many times, building awareness is counter-productive as resignation about environmental destruction is created. It is necessary to help the public understand what environment is to build the capacity of people to take the correct decisions about how they use resources. The problem is that we tend to speak to the same people, and they are already committed. We have to speak to new audiences and not allow those who are informed to become bored with environmental subjects. We need to know what we want to communicate and to whom. A communication strategy is required.

One problem is that conservationists may not know their objectives, and it is difficult to communicate what is not known. This is a conservationist's problem, not a communicator's one. Conservationists themselves need to be educated about how to communicate.

Discussion

The session was opened to comments from the audience, which addressed several topics:

❑ How to improve IUCN's role in relation to information and communication.

❑ How to narrow the distance between awareness and action and how to formulate a strategy to work with governments.

❑ How to convince donors to support information and communication projects.

❑ The need to educate journalists in environmental issues.

❑ The need to understand how to understand the role of information and communication at local community level.

❑ How to attract the general population towards environmental subjects with the same success of topics such as violence.

❑ How the press can influence the sustainable development paradigm.

❑ How to make publications more attractive to the public.

❑ How to include sustainability indicators.

In responding to these points, the panellists said:

❑ Providing financial assistance to reporters for an event like the WCC is a financial problem, not a philosophical one.

❑ Environmental consciousness is not just the concern of conservationists but of other sectors of the society too, and differs from one country to another. It is necessary to search for allies in new sectors like industry.

❑ Traditional knowledge should also be transmitted from local groups towards the outside. Local groups have a lot to teach conservationists.

❑ Though Internet means more communication, it also gives more power to those who have access to it and it finally turns elitist. Nobody can doubt the importance of Internet but it is not the final solution for everything.

❑ A challenge for communicators is the way to transmit news, to get a good story and reach a critical number of people.

❑ The way news is presented needs to be fundamentally reconsidered.

❑ The best sustainable indicators come from local organizations. There is not much information in relation to this.

In concluding, the Chair made three main points:

❑ Environmentalists should be more professional in communicating and must identify journalists who can help with information packaging. There must be official linkages with the press.

❑ Environmentalists should generate contacts with other sectors of society, with local groups, industry, etc.

❑ The important thing is to ensure that what we want to communicate actually reaches the correct media. It is necessary to pass from the awareness to the action stage. This cannot be done only by the press. We need to consider distribution, not only media production.

Special Event: Business and the Environment

Chair: Stephan Schmidheiny (Switzerland)

Panel members: William Ruckelshaus, Chief Executive Office, Browning-Ferris Industries, USA; Edgar Aseby, President and Chief Executive Officer, Andes Pharmaceuticals, Inc., USA; Jean Monty, President and Chief Executive Officer, Northern Telecom Ltd., Canada; Elizabeth Dowdeswell, Executive Director, UNEP

Rapporteur: Scott Hajost, IUCN-US

Introduction by the Chair

Stephan Schmidheiny, founder of the World Business Council for Sustainable Development, opened the session with an expression of gratitude to IUCN for including this session as part of the Congress. He then introduced the panellists and gave a brief opening statement commenting that people are critical/sceptical of business and the environment. He asked, what should motivate businesses? And how should business be better motivated?

Key issues in answering these questions include what customers demand, environmental laws, the activities of banks and insurance companies, and NGOs working through the media. Conservationists need to stimulate and challenge business and their employees, helping to convince them why they should be interested in conservation issues.

Forces working against business in this direction include market-distorting subsidies paid by governments; and consumer apathy and inertia.

He concluded with the interesting notion that business is an area where biodiversity is increasing.

Presentation by Panel Members

William Ruckelshaus made a number of key points:

❑ Individuals will pursue their own material well-being. How will this be pursued without harm to the environment?

❑ Business people should recognise that their self-interest is energy efficiency, which can lead to important cost savings.

❑ Businesses need to adopt policies consistent with laws, rules, training of individuals and incentives.

❑ Businesses should seek reasonable rules for corporate conduct, to ensure that all adhere to environmental policies. An agreed set of conditions or rules that are observed by all will ensure that no company unfairly benefits from ignoring environmental impacts of their activities.

❑ Social regulations need to protect health, safety and the environment. Society must define these rules for sustainable development, seeking a balance between demand and control. Economic incentives often work far better than regulations. Environmental goals must be aligned internationally to deal with global problems like acid rain and global warming, and locally, to deal with issues like recycling and waste management.

❑ We need to understand the conditions under which we operate. Good will alone will not achieve sustainable development. Government intervention is needed to ensure a level playing field.

Edgar Aseby answered the question, what is biodiversity prospecting? Today's world offers challenges and opportunities. The loss of biodiversity is a reflection of environmental crisis, but one way of dealing with the loss of biodiversity is to give it value for local people. One way of doing this is through bioprospecting. For example, 40% of prescriptions and 60% of anti-cancer drugs are derived from natural substances.

Finding an active substance in a plant is only the first step in a very long and expensive process to develop a marketable pharmaceutical, but in any case the source countries are not receiving enough benefits.

Firms like Andes Pharmaceuticals are seeking access in exchange for capacity building, recognizing that while the biotechnology is in the north, the biodiversity is in the south. Creating joint ventures helps to share risks and rewards, and building local capacity adds value to biological products in tropical countries. Creating an industry based on biodiversity serves the multiple goals of conserving biodiversity, improving the welfare of people living in areas with great species richness, and providing useful pharmaceuticals to all people.

Jean Monty pointed out that environment and its protection is good business, and therefore should be integrated into all processes. Corporate social responsibility is growing and the public is looking to business management to deliver on society's need for a healthy environment. This has paid off in terms of reduced costs and/or reduced consumption of resources, as well as elimination of CFCs in industrial processes. For example, NORTEL invested $1 million in environmental measures and saved $4 million, using a strategic business-like approach. By the year 2000 they will have reduced emission by 50%, paper by 30% and energy by 10%. They will spend $10 million and save four times that amount. This yields financial as well as environmental benefits.

Elizabeth Dowdeswell provided a perspective from the intergovernmental agency assigned responsibility for the environment. She noted that 1995 was not a good year for the environment and 1996 may not be much better. The evidence is that a world where 20% of the people are rich and 80% are poor is not sustainable.

Sustainability is not just about economics – it has critical social and environmental aspects as well. As the economy becomes increasingly globalized, the need for international cooperation is growing but the problems are growing even faster.

Global trade, often involving multinational corporations able to move their operations anywhere in search of lower costs and weaker environmental controls, gives us new challenges.

Innovation is needed in both technology and regulation, but the former is moving more quickly than the latter. Stronger regulations need to be joined by stronger incentives.

The role of business is critical, especially as the public is supporting greater environmental consciousness on the part of industry. We are now seeing the implementation of new approaches to dialogue and partnership, built on the linked concerns of business and consumers, adherence to standards of environmental efficiency, recognition of the critical role of business towards sustainability, and awareness that sound environmental practices are good for business.

Discussion

Comments from the audience included:

❑ Governments establish the conditions under which the private sector operates, and do not sufficiently penalize industry for environmentally irresponsible behaviour.

❑ Business is stimulated to do the right thing with incentives, including public recognition of such behaviour.

❑ Mandatory international standards are needed. For example, ISO 14000 offers a practical business tool for companies.

❑ We cannot wait for all governments to enforce environmental standards – greater action is needed from the environmental community to generate consumer demand for corporate environmental responsibility.

❑ Sustainable development is a three-legged stool, involving ecological, economic, and social/political elements. What is being done about the social aspects of sustainability?

In responding, the panellists made the following points:

❑ We have made a lot of progress since 1970, but we are not finished.

❑ No growth is no solution, but growth must be less material-intensive, reduce pollution emissions, and build in energy efficiency.

❑ We need a framework of international laws and regulations to incorporate incentives for technology transfer and encourage work with poor and developing countries as well.

In concluding, Stephan Schmidheiny made three points:

❑ Progress is visible; but more needs to be done in all parts of the world. Small and medium corporation have not been touched upon in this session but are critical elements in the mix.

❑ The environmental community needs to speak up and communicate with the private sector.

❑ We need more cooperation between the rich and poor countries of the world, which may have different priorities and values.

Special Event: Financing Sustainable Development

Chair: Maurice Strong

Panel members: Jean-François Rischard, World Bank; James Gustave Speth, Administrator of UNDP; Enrique Garcia, Andean Development Corporation; Tessa Tennant, NPI Global Care Investment

Rapporteur: Frank Vorhies, IUCN-HQ

Introduction by the Chair

This special plenary session opened with a statement from the chair, **Maurice Strong**, calling for innovative mechanisms to finance sustainable development. He noted that the world is moving beyond the period of foreign aid and that there is a lesson in this for IUCN.

Presentations by Panel Members

Jean-François Rischard warned that we need to link environment with development soon or the world would be headed for disaster. The challenge is how to get the private sector oriented to the environment and how to do it fast.

A strong correlation is now emerging between environmental success and economic success in the developing countries. This is because of (1) much tougher environmental regulations, (2) prices of energy rising to environmental prices, (3) open and fast information flows including inputs from NGOs and consumer groups, and (4) a fantastic financial industry that can invest quickly and easily.

Most developing countries lack these characteristics. Thus the job of the World Bank is to reinforce the institutional set-up for environmental management, remove the misguided subsidies on energy, etc. The job ahead is to create a relation between environmental success and economic success in developing countries.

James Gustave Speth noted that progress in the world is uneven and that over 100 developing countries are worse off now than they were five years ago. The massive private sector flows to the developing world go to only a few countries; over 80% ends up in 12 countries, 11 of which are middle income plus China.

Thus we need to join together in a campaign to sustain development cooperation. IUCN needs to join in the global partnership to reform development cooperation and to expand it because no substitute is available.

Enrique Garcia supported an integrated approach to sustainable development and explained that his organization is a good example of a new approach in the Latin America region. Its investments focus on infrastructure, including a biodiversity warning system, integration of micro-enterprises and eco-efficiency.

Tessa Tennant explained how her company is an active part of the UNEP insurance and environment initiative. They are identifying "green chip" companies, eco-efficiency, best practices in monitoring and so on. In short, they focus on capitalism for conservation. Further, the green investments are profitable. The green funds perform in the top 25%.

Since virtually everyone in the IUCN community has a bank account and perhaps 50% of them have pension funds, they need to ask what is happening with their own money and the money invested by their institutions. Five years ago, the Earth Summit at Rio issued a call to ensure that investment policies were promoting sustainable development. This call remains as important today as it was then.

Discussion

Maurice Strong led into the questions session by noting two clear streams in the presentations: general financing of sustainable development; and specific private sector sustainable development initiatives. The distinction is important as now less money is passing through the hands of government.

A wide variety of questions were raised during the questions from the floor including:

❏ military spending;

❏ the desire by the private sector for voluntary self-regulation;

❏ nuclear power in Canada;

❏ incremental costs;

❏ green accounting; and

❏ micro-enterprises, venture capital funds and national environmental funds.

The responses to these included:

❏ a call to bring UNEP out of its cocoon and to transform it into the World Environment Organization;

❏ sustainable development has to develop a financeable mode;

❏ IUCN has initiated a programme on greening national accounts;

❏ need to focus on the $ 1.5 trillion of investment and not just the $50 billion of aid flows;

❏ countries are mired in poverty and IUCN has championed moving people from poverty to save the environment; and

❏ we need to raise the level of financial literacy in developing countries.

Significant conclusions from this special session included:

❏ The world is moving beyond the period of significant foreign aid and there is an important message in this for IUCN.

❏ The challenge is how to get the private sector oriented to the environment and how to do it fast.

❏ The job ahead is to create a relation between environmental success and economic success.

❏ IUCN needs to join in a global partnership to reform development cooperation, including bringing UNEP out of its cocoon and transforming it into the World Environment Organization, and to expand it because no substitute is available, or on the horizon.

❏ The IUCN community should ask what is happening with its own money – its bank accounts, pension funds and investment funds – and ensure that these are promoting sustainable development.

Special Event: Nature in the 21st Century

Chair: Sir Martin W. Holdgate (UK)

Panel members: Sylvia Earle (USA); Edward Ayensu (Ghana); José Sarukhan (Mexico)

Rapporteurs: Leslie Wijesinghe, IUCN-Sri Lanka; and Jean-Yves Pirot, IUCN-HQ

Introduction by the Chair

Martin Holdgate introducing the subject from the Chair, stated that few issues are so central to IUCN's mission and mandate as the subject under discussion: the course of nature as we move into the 21st century. The future of humankind is inseparable from the future of nature, but damaging human impacts on natural systems are wide-ranging: stratospheric ozone depletion, climate change, desertification, deforestation, destruction of coral reefs, overfishing, and loss of species. The continuing increase in human population for at least the next 40 years is almost certain to exacerbate these environmental impacts further. Conservation science can help societies plan for the future and highlight possible pathways and key opportunities for action, especially in terms of policies.

The Chair emphasized that ecological processes are more dynamic and less predictable than assumed earlier, and human interventions are now increasing the rate of change. Consumption rates of natural resources are unsustainable in many areas. Extraction rates are many times higher than the natural rates of renewal. Human transport of species is breaking down biogeographical barriers and facilitating the spread of invasive species. Many of these impacts and degradation processes are unstoppable. To deal with issues we need to disaggregate and work at the community level because many of the problems vary from area to area. The future for nature in the 21st century will be the result of many local processes and interactions.

Presentations by Panel Members

Edward Ayensu spoke of the imperatives of development and conservation and the need to make them compatible. The 20th century has been marked by unprecedented industrial development and high population growth. In the developing world the prime strategic objective will continue to be economic growth, and this will be served by industrial growth which can provide the goods and services needed by most people. Economic growth in the South will affect Northern economies quite considerably, as the use of resources will become more equitable between the North and the South, and as industrialization will become more sensitive to local markets and conditions.

However, in pursuing industrial growth, the environment must be safeguarded in view of the importance of a healthy environment for sustainable development. Many industries in the developing world are wasteful of resources and cause heavy environmental pollution. The developed world on the other hand has created technologies that use resources economically and cause little pollution. These technologies have to be transferred to the developing countries, which will have to adopt improved standards for controlling industrial impacts, especially pollution. An essential condition for meeting these challenges is to ensure that governments and the private sector are committed to both economic development and environmental protection, the latter not being viewed as a luxury but rather as a requirement for long-term growth.

José Sarukhan spoke of the rate of change in natural systems that is occurring very rapidly today, and the need to use science to ensure that these changes do not cause serious damage to the environment, especially in the South where the rate of change is fastest. Science can play an important role in arresting environmental degradation and in guiding development and conservation options. Therefore, countries with high biodiversity should ensure that institutions and information systems are developed to collect and store data which can assist future decision making, as in Mexico (which ranks fifth on the list of the world's list of species richness) where a series of national and international institutions are working on the establishment of a comprehensive biodiversity information system. These data will be used in a scientific way to ensure that growth is compatible with conservation requirements.

Sylvia Earle referred to the oceans that cover 75% of the earth's surface as the earth's life support system. This system is stressed as never before. This century, billions of tons of fish and other life forms have been removed and billions of tons of toxic substances of all kinds have been dumped in the oceans. The most sophisticated fishing systems are being used to maximize the harvest of marine life, and the environmental cost of removing large amounts of resources on the functioning of the oceans is not taken into account ("We have a hard time thinking of fish as valuable unless they are dead"). In 1989, the annual catch of fisheries amounted to 90 million tons but this has declined steadily, showing that there is no surplus and that ecosystem productivity is being undermined. In our lifetime, 120 species of marine and fish have been placed under threat, and despite all our efforts, the giant whales may yet face extinction.

She stressed that we may use but should not use up the marine resources that are needed to support humanity. Without firm policies, fish resources will become rapidly extinct ("Fishing will be to our time what buffalo hunting was to the last century"), despite proven records that the fishery industry worldwide is so heavily subsidized that it is no longer economically profitable. Can humankind use its power to live peacefully with nature? Dr Earle stressed that the future of the oceans lies with all of those who feel concerned enough to try to influence the fisheries industry and existing government policies.

A special presentation was made by **Mr Yasuo Goto**, Chairman of the Keidanren Committee on Nature Conservation (Japan). The Keidanren is the Japanese Federation of Economic Organizations, which consists of over 1000 major private companies, and its Committee on Nature Conservation (now a member of IUCN) supports conservation projects in developing countries. Mr Goto spoke of the need for the private sector to contribute positively to the global environment, as businesses which will not be gentle to the environment in the 21st century will not succeed. The private sector must contribute to sustainable development by adopting an environmental philosophy based on a sense of modesty, and a spirit of gratitude and respect toward nature. This Keidanren philosophy, which is compatible with IUCN's philosophy for caring for the one and only Earth, must guide global citizens, including business management, in adapting our lifestyles to achieve sustainable development.

Discussion

A member of the audience summed up in one word ("greed") the problems that the world is facing today in conserving nature. Unless greed is monitored and this trend reversed, humankind has a bleak future. Another participant, while congratulating Dr Earle on her presentation, urged the conservation community to adopt a clearer definition of "sustainable use"; in response, the panel stated that land and water are there for us to use, but we should use these resources judiciously while continuing to do everything possible to halt the growth of the human population (it was stated that in 1700 years, at current rates of increase, the human mass would exceed the mass of the earth!). Technology can be used positively and negatively; new technologies offer a sign of hope, and education must be improved to assist communities in learning how not to degrade the environment.

In response to a question on protected areas in the marine environment, Dr Earle stated that the concept of protected areas for the oceans is relatively new. At present there are 1,200 marine sanctuaries, but they make up less than 1% of the open ocean area. We need to protect much more of the wild oceans and protection must be practised in the designated areas.

A member of the audience stated that the panellists dealt with the current trends and what needed to be done to reverse adverse trends, but he would have liked to see a perspective of what nature could look like 25 years from now compared to what we have today. Dr Ayensu, replying, stated that we cannot predict with any degree of certainty, however we can recognize the trends and take swift corrective actions, especially by transferring newly-developed technologies to the South. He also stressed the need to educate people, to increase land productivity, and to ensure that there is political will and commitment.

Another participant stated that often the lack of information is used as an excuse for the lack of political will. Professor Ayensu stated that the information industry will affect the people of the developing world and that poverty and civil strife would grow if there is no political will to pursue development.

A speaker from the floor stated that population pressure and economic development are there in the world today; what then would be the priorities for science for nature? In replying, the panel stated that a major contribution of science would be to assist putting the concept of sustainable development into practice. Another area where science has a distinct contribution to make is the marine environment. We know very little about the ocean and, therefore, we need to further explore the marine ecosystem and learn about it. As for scientific information, there will be more and better information and improved ways of using it.

A delegate from Australia, referring to the vast economic revolution taking place to the north of Australia, stated that technologies are needed to ensure that economic development in Asia would be sustainable. However, these technologies will have to be transferred from the developed countries.

A delegate from Canada stated that he would like to see Global Heritage Rivers established.

The Chair responding to a question on his advisory role in a dam construction project in Sarawak, stating that the government is going through with the project anyway. He had two options: either to dissociate himself from the project; or to advise on how the project could be accomplished with minimal environmental damage. In the light of this example, the Chair referred to the increasing urbanization the world over, and to the fact that new technologies will need to be used to design more efficient and environmentally friendly settlement structures, taking into account that 70-80% of the human population will soon be living in cities.

In summing up the debate, while regretting that participants focused more on the role of human societies instead of being predictive about trends in the natural world, the Chair listed the following issues that emerged during the discussion:

- ❑ The imperative of encouraging measures to halt human population growth and bring people into balance with the environment;

- ❑ The need to encourage a pattern of development that meets need rather than greed, and prevent inefficiency and waste;

- ❑ The need to address the pollution of poverty;

- ❑ The need to have lighter impacts on the sustaining earth;

- ❑ The need to develop and apply good science to the conservation and use of nature and natural resources;

- ❑ The need for sustainable use to be put into practice, through action, information, education, communication, etc.;

- ❑ The need for political will;

- ❑ The importance of the ethic set out in the World Charter for Nature, which promotes compassionate care for the earth and its natural resources;

- ❑ The need to develop an adequate protected area network, large enough to conserve life support systems and to allow evolutionary processes to continue.

The Chair concluded that "the human economy is a wholly owned subsidiary of human ecology. It is futile to expect science to save the world, but it is essential that science is available to play its appropriate part in that imperative of safeguarding nature and humanity".

Acknowledgements

Workshop 1.1 on Enhancing Sustainability: Resources For Our Future: We would like to express our gratitude to the Ford Foundation, Canadian Wildlife Service and the European Commission Directorate-General XI for their support to the Enhancing Sustainability: Resources for Our Future workshop.

Workshop 5.1 on Communications: The key to successful strategies, was supported by funds from Danish Development Cooperation, DANIDA; Directorate General for Development Cooperation, Italy; the Directorate General for International Cooperation, Netherlands and the Commission on Education and Communication Operation Fund.

Workshop 5.4 on Reaching Target Audiences and Changing Behaviour: Effective Communication in Strategies was supported by funds from Danish Development Cooperation, DANIDA; Directorate General for Development Cooperation, Italy; the Directorate General for International Cooperation, Netherlands and the Commission on Education and Communication Operation Fund.